CRA*f*TIVITY

40 PROJECTS FOR THE DIY LIFESTYLE

CRA*f*TIVITY

40 PROJECTS FOR THE DIY LIFESTYLE

TSIA CARSON

founder of SuperNaturale.com

A Lark Production

Collins
An Imprint of HarperCollinsPublishers

HarperCollins books may be purchased for educational, business, or sales promotional use. For information please write: Special Markets Department, HarperCollins Publishers, 10 East 53rd Street, New York, NY 10022.

FIRST EDITION

Designed by Flat

Library of Congress Cataloging-in-Publication Data has been applied for.

ISBN-10: 0-06-084130-3

ISBN-13: 978-0-06-084130-0

06 07 08 09 10 RRD 10   9   8   7   6   5   4   3   2   1

To Cedar

Introduction

Craftivity is a small window into the incredibly large and vital postmodern crafting community. It represents the creativity of its many contributors, people I have been friends with since I was a teenager and those I have met more recently by running an alternative DIY website called SuperNaturale. com. Every *Craftivity* project was made either by me or one of these individuals, not by professionals in some office park. The crafts are fun to make, eccentric, immediate, and occasionally profound. They often originated as gifts for friends, made for people, by people. They speak to the heart of craftivity.

WHY WE MAKE THINGS

I've always made things. Sometimes they are beautiful, sometimes they are useful, sometimes both, and sometimes neither. So I often wonder *why do we make things*?

Out of necessity? Rarely, I think. As a political statement? Well, the kind of agency one gains over their life by making their things is certainly powerful, heady stuff. But I can't honestly say that is *why* I make things. Do I make things for spiritual reasons? I wonder if I'm ready to speak of crafting as a form of meditation when I compare the crochet hats I make for my daughter's stuffed monkey to venerable practices like making Tibetan sand mandalas.

We make things for two reasons: pleasure and because we can. The pleasure is in the process and the end result is just a byproduct of this joy. This book can help you with the "because we can" part of the craftivity equation. It is for butterfly crafters, who flit from project to project, medium to medium, driven by some internal engine. Maybe you started as a kid by mending clothes, then learned how to really sew and use patterns. For late bloomers, craftivity almost inevitably begins with knitting, the gateway craft, and ends with something completely different like creating graffiti out of moss (see page 192). You begin with bejeweling table linens and end up with a loft bed. That's why the 40 projects are organized by material—fabric or glass—rather than a technique—silk screen or etching. Some projects you finish in an hour and others take a weekend. There are great things to wear, to put in your house or apartment, or to do with a partner. Crafters who are passionate about reusing items will find plenty of projects that involve recycling things around the house and using environmentally friendly materials.

People often think of crafting as the application of surface decoration—hot gluing gew gaws with abandon. Or following instructions for a project so that in the end it is about as inspired as coloring within the lines. Instead, I hope that you will consider these projects as a jumping off point for your own craftivity. Here are my tips, both practical and theoretical, before you begin.

GETTING STARTED

Do you believe in magic? Imagine creating something magical and full of surprise. Often that magic is the frisson that happens with a great craft concept—such as "I am going to make my old beloved t-shirts into underwear!" or "I can crochet a hat, why not a skull?" Sometimes it is easier to do this with someone in mind. What do they need? A blanket for their new baby? Candleholders made out of smoking pipes? Imagine the look on their face when you give it to them. That is how most of the projects in this book were invented.

Don't wear your craft on your sleeve. Living craftily doesn't mean that you make everything around you. Thoughtfully choose the things you are going to make. Before you make anything stop, drop and thrift; maybe you can get it second hand. I also love buying handmade things and thereby supporting other people's stuff. I make as little as possible, actually. The world is full of stuff. Only make the things that come out in sudden spasms of inspiration. Leave the rest alone.

Make mistakes and buy extra. I am the opposite of an expert crafter in all the crafts that I do. I make mistakes all the time. And that is just fine. The biggest mistake that I make is never buying extra. I live so in fear of waste that I always try to buy as little as possible of the materials I need and then I end up short. Don't do as I do.

SETTING UP

Here are the minimum supplies to have handy for *Craftivity*, a cookbook's standard ingredients list for your craft pantry. Gathering this stuff ahead of time shouldn't be hard—you probably already have a lot of it.

BASICS TO GATHER AND BUY

- A few types of glue (white, decoupage medium, epoxy, acrylic gel medium, wood)
- Gloves (work and rubber)
- Scissors for cloth and paper—the paper scissor can be inexpensive, the cloth—splurge on a nice bent #9. And never dull your cloth scissors with paper.
- Utility knife such as Exacto

- Tapes (masking, duct, scotch—you can never have enough tape)
- A pad of paper, some colored pencils and other writing implements come in handy
- A few small brushes (inexpensive, both bristle and foam)
- Tape measure
- Ruler
- Rubber cutting mat
- Twine and string
- Hammer
- Screwdrivers (regular and Phillips)
- Screws and anchors (wood, drywall)
- Needle-nose pliers
- Clippers (wire and garden)
- Nails (brads are almost always needed for something)
- Fine grit sandpaper
- Basic sewing supplies (needle set, straight pins, seam ripper, quality thread that doesn't snag—I love silk—a little bit of embroidery floss and yarn doesn't hurt either)
- A simple organizer for small items. This can be a plastic container with lots of compartments, a sewing box, baby food jars; I repurposed a Lazy Susan spice rack.
- An organizational method for larger items. I have a small dresser I pulled out of the trash for the big stuff.

NICE TO HAVE
- Glue gun with glue sticks
- Sewing machine (in good working order)
- Electric drill with bits
- A table saw

STUFF TO COLLECT AND SAVE
- Paper ephemera: old magazines, greeting cards, calendars and wrapping paper
- Scraps of fabric
- Unwearable sweaters
- Notions: ribbons, beads, buttons, pins, trims, rick rack
- Yarn and thread
- Interesting hardware: knobs, closures, hinges

PROTECT YOURSELF

Throughout this book I try to emphasize environmentally and therefore human friendly materials as well as using protective gear. Please take heed. Gloves and goggles are indispensable to protecting you physically. Also be sure to work in well-ventilated areas. Chemical odors, even drying house paint, are noxious. Wear face masks and respirators—fine particulate matter can wreak havoc on your lungs. Please keep your crafting and cooking materials separate.

KEEPING UP

Keep an inspiration file. Get a folder or box. When you see something that you love in a magazine rip it out and put it in your file. Or take a photo. Keep a folder on your computer and a bookmark folder in your web browser for this as well—when you see something cool, grab the image or make a bookmark. If you take digital pictures be sure to keep your snaps around of things you think are interesting. Then on a rainy day you can just browse.

Keep a blog. But only if you are really into sharing. You can put your stuff up on a blog site or on a picture sharing site. You not only get feedback but also keep a record of what you do. Often we don't take the time to document our own stuff. You will also inevitably find like-minded crafters and this will broaden your community and inspiration.

Throw things away. My grandmother was a pack rat. Every drawer in her house was filled with stuff, you would open one drawer and it was full of kewpie dolls. More dolls than anyone could need. The next drawer was filled with empty aspirin bottles. You know what happened to this stuff? Nothing. And eventually it had to be hauled out of there. Don't be my grandmother. Give it away to friends, swap it online at SuperNaturale.com, donate it to a thrift store or just throw it out.

Buying supplies. Craft stores are dangerous places. So is eBay. Everything can look gorgeous and a must have. Here is my recommendation. Begin with an idea. Make a list. Then walk into that store or surf the web. Stick to your list; but make a note of anything else you like. If you live near a metropolis or will be visiting one find out where the notion and trimmings stores are. You can look on SuperNaturale.com, and use the yellow pages. Make a budget and divide it roughly by stores you will go into. Give yourself an afternoon and look in all of the stores. Buy what you want within your budget. Make a note of other things. Take business cards. Take photos if they allow. This will help you when you are looking for a special something.

Tips for successful long-term craftivity. You will only do the things you love. If you can find some kind of creative outlet that gives you pleasure you will never stop doing it or learning from it. Sometime we need to take a break from making things but inevitably we will get that urge to make again. You have a lifetime of making ahead of you. Enjoy each moment.

HOW TO USE THIS BOOK

The six sections are Yarn and String, Fabric and Thread, Paper and Plastic, Glass and Ceramics, Wood and Metal, and Lost and Found. Projects within each section follow a learning curve beginning with the easiest, *Craft Lite*, and ending with the most challenging, *Craft Master*. In between are *Craft Luxe* projects. If a project involves a specific craft technique, it's cross referenced to a *Craftshop*, which gives you the basic knowledge you need to complete the project. Craftshops include knitting, crochet, spinning, felting, stitchery, silk screen, ceramics, wood, and hardware. If a hard-to-find or uncommon material is listed, I've included a resource for obtaining it in the appendix on page 222. Occasionally, I just show you amazing works of art and craft. Called *Showcase*, they are meant as pure inspiration, not as something you would try to make yourself.

SUPERNATURALE.COM

You can also visit the SuperNaturale.com website where you can find lots of extra information, interviews with the makers, all the patterns in printable digital format and assorted errata.

YARN STRING

part 1

Kool Aid Yarn

Dyeing wool with unsweetened Kool Aid is a fun easy way to make beautiful, vibrant yarn, and it makes an excellent gift for your knitter friends. It's best to start with a white all wool yarn. White yarn gives you a clear idea of what color each packet of Kool Aid will yield. Wool is a good yarn because it's relatively inexpensive and absorbs dye readily. Acrylic and cotton yarns don't give good results with Kool Aid dyes.

You'll Need:

A large non-reactive stainless steel or enamel stockpot (avoid aluminum)

3 or 4 small, individual, unsweetened Kool Aid packs per skein of wool. A good ratio is an ounce of Kool Aid per ounce of wool.

White vinegar

Plastic or other disposable cup

A face mask

Crystal Palace Labrador and Iceland undyed wool hanks, loosely tied

Learning which flavors make good colors is trial and error—some are duds. My personal favorites are black cherry, lime, orange, and lemonade. Kool Aid blue, for example, is a tough one—it doesn't make an intense blue.

Lighter shades like lemonade require two or three packets of Kool Aid to give a rich enough color to the yarn. I adjust lemonade with a dash of lime or orange to get a color I like. This is the fun part so mix up colors you love. Start out light and go gradually darker. If you put too many colors of contrasting hues together you may get a muddy color. Nothing ventured, nothing gained. You've only got a package or two of Kool Aid at stake here. If you want overall uniform color in the skein you should add the color to the water before you add the (soaked) yarn. If you like variegated effects, put the dye in after the skein is in the dye pot. I like adding dye as the pot begins to simmer—stirring gently to keep the dye even. I also pour the Kool Aid mix directly onto sections of the wool in the water to have areas where the dye is stronger than others.

The scientists among us measure amounts and record results carefully—and this can be done with Kool Aid dyeing—but yours truly is an approximator who measure with "more or less" and "about" units. I like the unknown and the unexpected. Fear not, there's fun and good results to be had whatever your measuring style.

MAKING IT

1. Cover the wool skein with an ample amount of water and 1/2 cup white vinegar, and soak in the stockpot until it's fully absorbed all the water (about 30 minutes). (Try one skein at a time till you get a sense of what Kool Aid flavors make which colors.)

2. Put on your face mask. Even though it smells good, the dust from the Kool Aid is very fine and just like regular dye, you do not want it in your lungs as it can cause respiratory discomfort. Also, Kool Aid has dye in it, so it will leave color on your counter and on your hands. While it's not a permanent dye, use gloves and cover the counter with newspaper to keep the clean up fast.

3. Stir part of a packet of Kool Aid, 3/4 cup of water, and 1 to 2 tablespoons white vinegar in a disposable cup. As I like to mix colors, I use only part of 2 or 3 Kool Aid packages.

4. Put the pot on the range and set it to simmer. Once it achieves a low simmer, it will be "cooked" in about 30 minutes.

5. At first the water will be a cloudy version of the color you have mixed up. When the water becomes clear, that's the sign that the dye has locked into the yarn fiber. Let the pot cool down gradually before attempting to remove the yarn.

6. Rinse skein gently with fresh water. Use a wool wash or a revitalizing shampoo followed by a conditioner to take the Kool Aid residue and vinegar out of the fibers.

7. Roll in a towel, squeeze and hang skein to dry.

CRAFT MORE

✤ Steaming is an alternative dye method. Cover a counter top with plastic wrap or a garbage bag. Lay the presoaked skein on top of the plastic. This is a process that can be used with single or multiple colors. Drip or pour Kool Aid mixed with water and vinegar as described above on the skein. You can use several different color mixtures. Wrap the plastic around the skein, envelope style, and steam in a covered steamer for 30 to 45 minutes. Be especially careful not to lift the steamer's lid till the pot has cooled as the cool air can cause felting, and of course, the contents are very hot. So allow plenty of time for things to cool to avoid being burned. Rinse your beautiful yarn with wool wash or shampoo as described above.

✤ Overdyeing, a technique in which you re-dye to change a color to a new shade, is also fun once you know how to get the colors you like. You can overdye a yarn the same color to increase intensity—to even take a light color into a different color. Remember to go from light yarn to dark, as dyes are not strong enough to have much effect on dark colors.

Spinning and Recycled Yarn

A yarn habit can be really expensive. Here are some ways to save cash and at the same time earn crafting extra credit.

SPINNING YARN

The wonder of making your own wool yarn is that it's formed by the simplest of processes. The fibers that make up the raw wool grab onto each other when twisted and form yarn.

To make wool yarn you could start at the very beginning with the shearing of the sheep. The resulting fleece is matted with the debris of months of outdoor living and oily with a heavy lanolin. After these gnarly locks are scoured and cleaned, the wool is then carded to take the gnarls out and to align the fibers. These clean little rolls of wool, called roving, are ready to spin into yarn. I recommend skipping over the wool prep and starting with wool roving so you can get right down to spinning essentials. It's easier to spin fibers that have been prepared and catching the hang of the right twist and draft is your first objective. Roving is easily bought online or at your local specialty yarn shop.

SPINNING

Spin your own yarn and a whole new world of options opens before you. Not only can you play with the size and weight of the yarn, you can combine fibers in innovative ways that you can't find in stores. Once you get going you can start mixing up exotic fiber concoctions that include zany bits of everything but the kitchen sink.

THE SPINDLE

To spin, you need a spindle. You can buy a hand spindle for about $15 online. Or you could spend a lot more for a spinning wheel, which is a big commitment for a newbie spinner. So if you are trying this out, go the low risk route and look for a spindle known as a bottom-whorl drop spindle.

TWIST AND SPIN

And now, to spin! Holding the spindle with the whorl on bottom, wind a piece of yarn (your "leader") about a foot long around the dowel, or "shaft," near the whorl. You could secure it with a half hitch knot. Bring it up and loop it through the hook. Feather out the ends of the leader. Hold a handful of roving fibers, feather the ends of them also, and overlap them with the yarn leader. Here's the tricky bit: with one hand, spin the shaft of the spindle, letting it drop and spin freely, and pinch the roving fiber and yarn leader together; with the other, slowly let out the fiber as it twists into yarn. Bear in mind that the spindle must always spin in the same direction, or your yarn will unwind. Also, the amount of fiber you let out determines the thickness of your yarn. Spin until your spindle hits the ground, then wind your yarn around the shaft until you have about a foot left to serve as your new leader. Put the yarn through the hook and start spinning again. When the spindle starts wobbling, you have enough yarn: unwind it from the shaft. Prepare your yarn as described below.

In spinning there's a Z twist (clockwise) and an S twist (counterclockwise).

It doesn't matter which one you choose—both make equally good yarn. And once you've mastered the basic twist and spin, there's more fun to come: plying. Plying allows you to twist two or more yarns together. The two yarns being plied must twist in opposite directions, otherwise you'll unspin the yarn you've already made. One must be an S and one must be a Z. Plying is a blast if you use very different yarns together to get creative combinations. Machines cannot make this kind of yarn—only you can. Qualities in manufactured yarns that are considered "flaws" like being overtwisted, uneven, or too bulky become stunning in a hand spun yarn.

Once you get the hang of a drop spindle, you may be sufficiently entranced to try a spinning wheel. Using a spinning wheel is relaxing and breezy. It's like using an old-fashioned treadle sewing machine —you're the energy source and you set the pace.

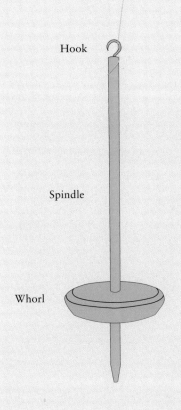

Hook

Spindle

Whorl

One hundred percent cotton and wool—lamb's wool, alpaca, or cashmere—are all solid yarns worth recycling. Make sure you can knit with the gauge. Worsted or a bulky weight is best. Really small gauge yarns mean days of rewinding yarn to reskein, wash and reball it.

Cut the thread inside the seams to separate out the pieces of your target sweater. A serged seam or two, most likely at the top of the shoulder, might be salvaged with a lot of work, but feel free to just cut the darn thing out. As you cut out the seams, find your yarn ends, and unravel as you would when knitting yarn on needles. Sweaters are usually knit bottom to top, so unravel top to bottom. Try to keep it free of tangles. Once the yarn is liberated, you're ready to get it into some usable form.

RECYCLED YARN

Keeping your yarn stash healthy doesn't always mean buying retail. Recycled yarn is a bargain that makes you feel good about reusing resources. Reused yarn has also got a great feel to it, what's called a great hand, if you pick your project carefully. Recycled cotton for example is extremely soft.

All those sweaters on your shelves that don't fit quite right, all the cute thrift shop items that are completely not your style—gather them up and turn them into something new.

First, check the seams of the items you're considering. Any garment with mostly machine-serged seams is going to come out as a million yard-long pieces of yarn. You want seams that are sewn to finished edges rather than heavy threads covering cut ends.

Don't settle for beat up or worn sweaters. If the yarn has been abused, it won't be worth the effort you put into recycling it. Be extra careful to check Fair Isle knits because its inside stranding may wear out secretly, with no hint of it on the outside.

GETTING READY

Wrap the yarn around your arm, elbow to palm, to make a skein. To set the skein and reduce curl in the yarn, fill a tub with warm water, add mild detergent, and leave the yarn in for a few minutes. Rinse, then dry by squeezing gently with a towel. If your skein is still curly, hang it to dry and put a weight (not too heavy, you'll stretch it) on the bottom to straighten it out a bit. To turn your skein into a center-pull ball, start with a 6-inch tail, which you'll hold onto with your thumb. Wrap around your thumb and pinky in a figure-eight pattern about ten times. Then take your fingers out of the two halves, mush them together, and, holding the mushed ball in your fingers, wrap the yarn around your fingers and the ball about ten times, making sure to keep track of the pull with your thumb. Switch your fingers so they're perpendicular to where they were at first, and wrap ten more times. Then take your fingers out and wrap normally but loosely. Fish out your 6-inch pull, conveniently located by your thumb, and you've got a ball.

Pom-Pom Rug

BY LANA LÊ

This plush pom-pom rug was inspired by the wooly shag rugs from the '60s. It's a quick and simple way to create fuzzy cover underfoot, and use up any leftover yarn from previous projects. How much yarn varies since there's no gauge and the size and shape is up to you. There are basically two components to the rug: the pom-poms and the base. The base is the shape that the pom-poms are tied or sewn onto. We recommend that you make a base the desired size and shape and then produce as many pom-poms as necessary to cover it. If you don't know how to knit or crochet or want to save time, you can use a blanket or piece of fabric as the base.

Diagram A

You'll Need:

(For the 48" diameter rug shown)

8 balls Lion Brand Wool-Ease Thick & Quick, approximately 864 yards total, color pewter

Scrap piece of cardboard

Size N (10 mm) crochet hook

Scissors

Pom-poms: 26 balls Knit Picks' Wool of the Andes, approximately 2,626 yards total, in the following colors: pumpkin, chocolate, maple syrup, tomato, avocado, asparagus, carrot, cherry blossom, red, iron ore, cranberry, hollyberry, mulled wine, wheat; 20 balls Brown Sheep's Lamb's Pride, approximately 2,125 yards total, in the following colors: fuchsia, ruby red, wild violet, orchid thistle, seafoam, kiwi, prairie fire, pistachio, blue heirloom, and sable

The rug offers endless possibilities for creativity and individuality. Fibers, weights, ply or non-ply yarns will look and perform differently. Try making pom-poms with wool, cotton, and mixed fibers to see which you prefer. Don't be afraid to experiment with monochromatic or bold color combinations; vary the size or make multi-colored pom-poms. You can change the overall shape or attach several shapes or pieces together. Cover the rug completely with pom-poms or spread them apart. Arrange the pom-poms in different patterns or leave part of the base exposed.

This pattern is easy peasy. Gather a group of pals together and have a pom-pom party to make things go faster. The rug shown here took about 24 hours to make spread out over two weeks and with the assistance of a few friends.

Kids cannot resist crawling on this rug and it will bring a smile to anyone lucky enough to receive it as a gift.

MAKING IT

1. Start with a base. Using a chunky yarn, double crochet a circular base. (I used the Wool-Ease Thick & Quick for the base.) Chain 7 and slip stitch for the first round. Increase every round until you have a flat circle, 4' in diameter. (See Crochet Craftshop on page 39.)

2. Make the pom-poms. With a sharp pair of scissors, trim a piece of cardboard into a 3" w x 2" h rectangle. Then cut a 1/2" notch in the center of each of the short sides of the card.

3. Cut a length of yarn about 10 to 11" and secure it across the width of the cardboard by tucking it into the notches. This will be the pom-pom tie.

4. Continue by taking yarn from the skein, and winding it around the card over the pom-pom tie. The amount of times you wrap the yarn will depend upon the thickness of the fiber, and affects the fullness of the pom-pom, so you may want to experiment. I wrapped the Lamb's Pride Bulky about 70-80 times, and the Wool of the Andes approximately 120 times.

5. Detach the pom-pom tie from the notches and make a tight square knot around the wrapped yarn (see diagram A). Turn the card over to the opposite side, and cut the wrapped yarn through the middle, trimming off the end connected to the skein at the same time.

6. Adjust the strands so that they are securely centered within the knotted tie, and fluff slightly by shaking the pom-pom while holding the long ends of the tie or combing the strands with your fingers.

This method creates graduated pom-poms that have shorter strands near the center and longer ones toward the bottom, much like a chrysanthemum flower. The pom-poms should be fuller than tassels, yet not ball-shaped, like traditional pom-poms, making them more comfortable to tread on.

7. Assemble the rug once you've made enough pom-poms. Arrange them on top of the base in the desired pattern and tie them to the base using the long ends of the knotted tie. Finish by trimming the ends of the pom-pom ties. If the rug seems too fragile, sew through the center of each pom-pom with more yarn or thread, further securing them to the base.

CRAFT MORE

✤ You could knit the base, or use a heavy blanket or cloth.

✤ Experiment with lightly felting this rug to make it more durable for cleaning. (See page 82 for felting instructions.) Or use it as a throw instead of a rug.

Knitting

People used to decode knitted objects by unraveling them. They were just guessing at what you were supposed to do. Hence the difference in knitting styles and approaches. People on the continent slipped the yarn through their left hand as they knit. People in the British Isles threw their yarn over their needles.

Now we are blessed with knitting patterns but has this helped us to knit any better? Are we now truly one with our knitting needles? The knitted object is a text you can read. It can tell you almost all you need to know. Learning to knit is a little like learning to write. A cabled sweater is like a dense book—sure, you might need in-depth knowledge to understand it. The projects in this book, however, are more like haikus or limericks, short and easy to remember. No worries.

KNITTING NEEDLES

Long straight needles are what the average knitter starts out with—they're the traditional needles that you think of when you hear the word "knitting." Needles come in various materials, from plastic to bamboo to metal, and are sized by number, from 1 to 50. In the past, however, there have been some discrepancies in sizing, so the safest way to choose a needle is by metric size, or how many millimeters it's labeled. Circular needles consist of two short straight needles connected by a long, flexible piece of plastic or metal. They are useful for big projects and for knitting in the round—tube-like things like sweaters with no seams.

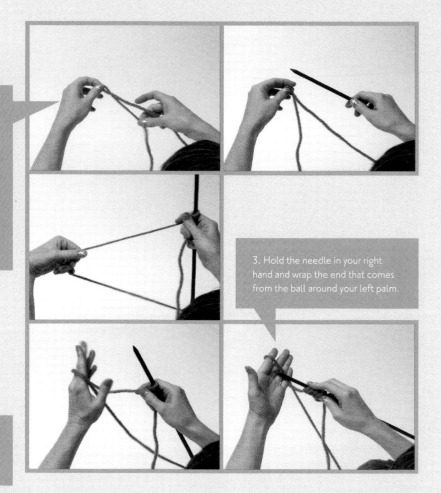

1. Knitting patterns begin with the number of stitches to cast on. So measure a tail of 1/2-inch to 1-inch of yarn for each stitch you need to cast on.

2. Make a slip knot on the needle: loop the tail end of the yarn over the ball end, pull the tail through the loop, put the needle in the loop, and pull tight (but not too tight).

3. Hold the needle in your right hand and wrap the end that comes from the ball around your left palm.

4. Push the tip of the right needle up through the loop wrapped around your left palm.

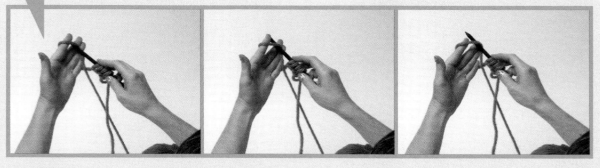

Cast On: Casting on, the first step in knitting, is how you get the yarn on the needle. There are several ways to cast on, but we'll be using the simplest method, the Single Cast On.

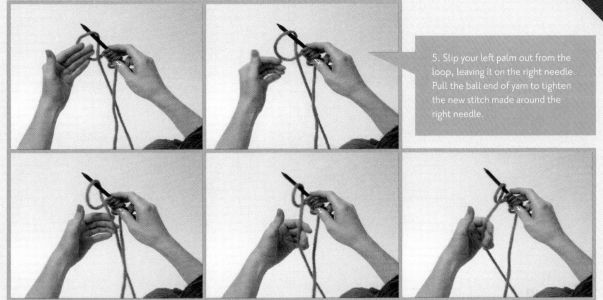

5. Slip your left palm out from the loop, leaving it on the right needle. Pull the ball end of yarn to tighten the new stitch made around the right needle.

6. Repeat steps 2 through 5 until you have the proper number of stitches for your project. Try not to pull the yarn too tight, so you'll have some give for your next row. As you knit the next row, extra yarn will accumulate from each stitch. That's fine. You'll just have a long tail of extra yarn at the end of the row.

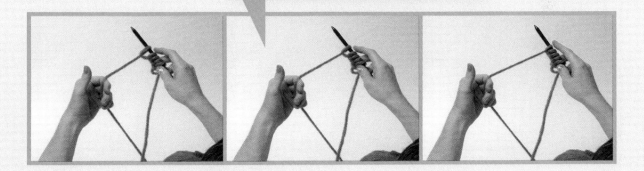

1. Start with the empty needle in your right hand, and the yarn and needle with cast-on stitches in your left.

2. Slide the tip of the empty needle, left to right, from the front to back of the left needle, and through the loop of the first cast-on stitch. The needles will cross in the back, with the right needle behind the left.

3. Loop the yarn counterclockwise around the empty needle witvh your left index finger. Push the needle down and through the stitch, carrying the new loop.

Knit: The knit stitch is your most basic. The two most common ways to hold your needle for the knit stitch are the English and Continental styles. Although many knitters prefer English, I like the Continental style because it's easier for beginners.

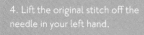

4. Lift the original stitch off the needle in your left hand.

5. Repeat steps 2 through 4 until you've finished a row—then switch the needles to your opposite hands and start again.

1. Push the needle in your right hand down through the first stitch, right to left, towards you and in front of the left needle.

2. Drape the yarn over the tip of the empty needle counterclockwise.

3. Pull the empty needle back through the stitch, taking the new loop with it.

Purl: The purl stitch is almost as essential as the knit stitch, and luckily it's almost as easy: just remember to carry the yarn in the front instead of the back.

4. Lift the original stitch off the needle in your left hand.

5. Repeat steps 2 through 5 until you've purled a whole row.

Needle Conversion Chart

METRIC	KNITTING USA	KNITTING UK
2	0	14
2.25	I	13
2.75	2	12
3		11
3.25	3	10
3.5	4	
3.75	5	9
4	6	
4.5	7	7
5	8	6
5.5	9	5
6	10	4
6.5	10.5	3
7		2
8	11	0
9	13	00
10	15	000
11.5		
12.75	17	
15	19	
16		
19	35	
25	50	

BIND OFF

Binding off is a tidy way to end your project and get it off the needle. Once you know the knit stitch, it's a cinch.

1. At the beginning of a row, knit two stitches.

2. Slide the left needle into the first stitch on the right needle.

3. Pull the first stitch over the second stitch and off the right needle, leaving the second stitch on.

4. Knit another stitch. You should now have two stitches on your right needle and one bound-off stitch.

5. Repeat steps 2 through 4 until you're done with the row and all your stitches but one are bound off.

6. Cut the yarn, leaving a short tail, and thread the tail through the last stitch. Slip it off the needle and pull the thread to knot the stitch. All done!

BEYOND THE BASICS

Knowing how to knit and purl gives you a foundation for almost all common stitches. Even complex patterns are usually just combinations of these two basics. The garter stitch is the simplest, using only the knit stitch. Stockinette is the next level up: knit one row, purl one row all the way through. Ribbing is useful for the edges of sweaters and hats, since it stays tight. To make a rib stitch, knit one or more stitches, then purl the same number of stitches and repeat for the length of the row, ending with purl stitches. Repeat every row to make vertical columns of rib. A moss or seed stitch looks like a little checkerboard: knit one, purl one for a whole row, ending with a knit, then start the next row by knitting one, so that each "column" of stitches alternates knit and purl. I hope this demystifies these useful stitches for you.

CHANGING YARN

Like most knitting basics, changing yarn is not as hard as it looks. Stranding, or Fair Isle, is the easiest way to change yarn in the middle of a project or a row. Just twist the new yarn around the strand of yarn being used and start knitting with the new color only. Carry the old color, loosely, in the back, ready to be used again. Make sure each color is 5 or less stitches, so you don't have long strands drooping and getting tangled. Keep the loose strands in back of the work, so for the finished project it's on the inside of your sweater, hat, or whatnot.

The Method Scarf

BY JOHANNA BURKE

I was a slow learner with knitting. In fact, after years of experience, I am still basically making hats and scarves and need considerable coaching when the shaping part begins. One thing I am really great at, however, is finding and buying beautiful yarns! Years ago, as Christmas approached, the annual crafter's dread consumed me: Gifts were in order. I surveyed my empire of colored, textured, and novelty yarns and realized that at the speed I was knitting, I would have half a hat by Christmas. I would be a very old woman by the time I mastered the soft and beautiful mohair I so longed to knit with. Something had to be done, and "the method" was the answer.

You'll Need:

Lots of yarn, in a variety of weights, colors, and textures

Size 19, 35, or 50 (15, 19, or 25 mm) knitting needles

Size J-Q (6-16 mm) crochet hooks

Scissors

Beading a ball of yarn.

To work the method, a number of yarns are combined to make one fat multi-textured strand that is knitted together with big funny-looking needles. Knitting in this big size will allow you to complete things fast—and, if you have a yarn-collecting problem, to trim the fat from your stash. Remember, there are all sorts of ways to blend yarns—what makes the method yours is the free choice and abuse of colors and yarns yielding unexpected results.

Lots of strands of yarn equal thick stitches. Often a method scarf will only need 10 stitches or less for width. Spend time working on your colors and try things you don't expect to look right. Monochrome can look cool, for example.

Although you are blending colors and textures, your end project will still be a combination of the parts. You cannot turn an excess of acrylic into cashmere—acrylic will dominate the blend, so use with awareness. Similarly, do not use a high-quality soft yarn with lesser yarns if you are going for soft. This is a great place to mix in the mohair that is too fine to knit solo. The alchemy of the method is in the color and mixing.

As for knitting needles, the bigger the better. The biggest needles give you the loosest knit, which generally is best because it makes the scarf more pliable and flat when worn. If the knit is too tight the scarf becomes stiff and uncomfortable.

MAKING IT

1. Gather your yarns together. They must be knit-ready—either in balls or in pull-skeins.

2. Grab about 4 strands of different yarns and twist them together for about 5". This will give you a feeling for the colors together. Add other colors if you'd like.

3. Make a swatch. This is how you confirm your combinations of colors, while simultaneously deciding which needle size is best. Start with a large needle and cast on 4 or 6 stitches. Knit up a few rows to see how it will look. When you arrive at your desired combination, you have a gauge to work with. I often spend a lot of time on the swatches.

4. Once you have chosen your colors, place your yarns in a bag or other snag-free container. Grab the strands from each bag together to create your special chunky yarn combination. Work on your knitting at about three feet away from the bags so the yarns have a chance to straighten and combine before they reach the piece.

Here are three examples of scarves created by novice knitters and crocheters.

GINGKO

1. Thread all the yellow beads with a yarn needle onto the merino stripe ball.
2. With all three yarns at once, cast on 3 stitches with size 50 needles.
3. Knit every row, and space beads randomly, threading them in as you knit.
4. When you run out of beads, bind off. Scarf will be approximately 20' long.
5. Add fringe to each short end with all three yarns.

You'll Need:

I ball Crystal Palace Labrador, color limeade

I ball each Crystal Palace Kid Merino, colors fern mix and kiwi

I ball Crystal Palace Merino Stripes, color sandstorm

I package yellow pastel pony beads

I pair size 50 (25 mm) knitting needles

MALIBU

1. Thread beads with a yarn needle onto one of the thinner yarns (the Rowan Yarns Wool Cotton or the Jaeger Extra Fine Merino).
2. With all four yarns held together, cast on 5 stitches with 50 (25 mm) needles.
3. Knit in knit stitch and space beads randomly.
4. At 75 rows, bind off.
5. Add fringe made of all four yarns to each short end.

You'll Need:

I ball Rowan Yarns Big Wool, color sugar spun

I ball Rowan Yarns Soft Lux, color cashmere

I ball Rowan Scottish Tweed 4 Ply, color thatch

I ball Jaeger Extra Fine Merino DK, color tweed

Large-holed faceted clear plastic beads, any size you like (2 packs of 60 count)

I pair size 50 (25 mm) knitting needles

SPARROW

1. With all yarns held together, chain 6.
2. Work in double crochet until the shortest ball ends.
3. Add fringe made from all yarns to each short end.

You'll Need:

I ball Jaeger Extra Fine Merino DK, color badger and cypress (or use Rowan Yarns Cashsoft Aran, color bud)

I ball Rowan Yarns Kidsilk Night, color moonlight

Size Q (16 mm) crochet hook

Knit Lampshade

I admit it. I almost tossed this thing out the window. It was one of those craft projects where you have this whole fantasy of what would look good and how easy it would be to make. The kind where your loved ones give you blank looks as you show them all the raw materials. I would swatch something up and put it up to the lampshade and think—this just isn't right. And I would have to start all over again. You'd never know by looking at it, it seems so casual. That is its genius.

You'll Need:

I ball Lion Brand Glitterspun, color gold

I ball Lion Brand Moonlight Mohair, color safari

A lampshade (I used a bell-shaped linen lampshade, 10" at top diameter, 14" at bottom diameter, 10 1/2" high)

I pair size 15 (10 mm) knitting needles

Tapestry needle

A pretty pin or brooch (even the kind of safety pin you use for a tartan skirt would look nice, very '80s)

Gauge: 10 stitches x 15 1/2 rows = 4"

As I was trying to wrap this thing around my lampshade again to see if I had finally gotten it right I realized my whole elaborate way of lacing it was just not going to work. In fact it was pulling apart my stitches. I cursed under my breath. I ran over to my totally disorganized supply area and found a little cache of antique pins I had been saving. Maybe this will work, I thought. I took one and put it through just to hold the knitting in place while I figured out what to do next. I took one look at it and realized there was no "next." It was perfectly placed. It was done, as if by magic.

Now honestly, I hate to be told what to do. If you are like me, you can be loose with following this pattern. And the cover does not need to fit your shade precisely in order to look good. In fact it looks better if it doesn't. In other words you can't go wrong.

MAKING IT

I. Measure the circumference of your shade both top and bottom. Measure the height. My shade was 10 1/2" high with 31 1/2" top circumference and 44" bottom circumference. You can adjust this pattern based on the gauge.

You knit the piece about an inch higher than the actual lampshade measurements. So I made my piece 14" long. Knit a nice loose stockinette stitch so it will have a lot of stretch. Begin your pattern with the largest circumference. The pattern for my piece is as follows, but I feel like you can place stripes as you see fit. It is great to have them be thin, fuzzy and widely spaced. Hold your work up to the shade as you knit to make sure things are right. I think what makes this one look so great is the stripe placed along the bottom of the shade.

ADAPT AS YOUR LAMPSHADE REQUIRES:

Cast on 120 stitches in the Glitterspun gold.
Work in stockinette stitch (knit one row, purl one row) starting with a purl row for 3 rows.
Row 4: Decrease 6 stitches evenly across row. Work for 5 more rows.
Rows 10-11: Change to Moonlight Mohair safari and continue in stockinette stitch.

Row 12: Change to Glitterspun gold, continue in stockinette stitch but decrease 6 stitches evenly across row. Work for another 7 rows.
Row 20: Decrease 6 stitches evenly across row. Work for another 7 rows.
Row 28: Decrease 6 stitches evenly across row. Work for another 3 rows.
Rows 32-33: Change to Moonlight Mohair safari and continue in stockinette stitch.
Row 34: Change to Glitterspun gold, continue in stockinette stitch. Work for 1 more row.
Row 36: Decrease 6 stitches evenly across row. Work for 7 rows.
Rows 44-45: Change to Moonlight Mohair safari and continue in stockinette. In row 44 only, decrease 6 stitches evenly across row. Work for 6 more rows.
Row 52: Decrease 6 stitches evenly across row.
Row 53: Purl.
Row 54: Knit, decreasing another 6 stitches (72 stitches across).
Row 55: Bind off.

2. Using a tapestry needle, thread a piece of yarn through the top row or two so that it hugs the lampshade tightly. Tie a small bow.

3. Find a spot towards the bottom of your shade to pin together the rest of your shade. Adjust the knitting as needed. I pulled mine lengthwise so that it comes down below the shade.

Crochet

Some knitters treat crochet like the Cinderella of craftivity. "Well," the haughty woman at the yarn shop informed me, "any knitter can crochet, but not all crocheters can knit." What is it about crochet that enrages knitters? Is it that they secretly know knitting needles originally had hooks on the end of them? Is it jealousy as their work inevitably slides off their needles while we just have to keep that leading loop on?

Crochet is not knitting. Crochet is sculpture. Crochet is concrete. It allows us to see what we are making as we are making it. It allows us to take the two-dimensional strand of yarn and create forms in three-dimensional space. Let's use crochet for what crochet is good for and not compare it to anything else.

SUPPLIES

The biggest difference between knitting and crochet is in the hook—crochet hooks, as opposed to knitting needles, are sized by letter instead of number, from B (the smallest) to about Q (the largest). Like knitting needles, rely on a hook's metric size if in doubt. Make sure your hook and yarn together come out to the right gauge for your project. And you should know that it takes more yarn to crochet than to knit any given item—don't ask why cause I don't know.

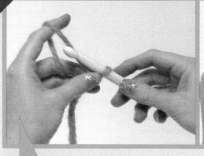

1. Make a slipknot around your crochet hook.

2. Holding the tail end taut in your left hand, push the hook in front of the ball end of the yarn, then under and around it, making a loop on the hook.

3. Pull the loop you've just made through the slipknot and out. You now have one stitch made and one loop on your hook. Repeat steps 2 and 3 for however many chain stitches your pattern requires. You've just made a foundation chain.

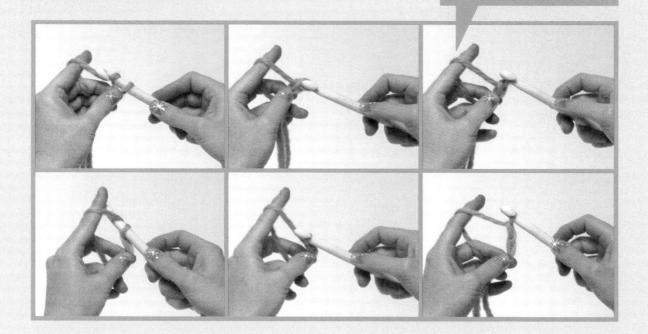

Foundation chain: As the name implies, this is where it all begins. Chain stitches might remind you of the lanyard you used to play with at summer camp—just yarn instead of plastic.

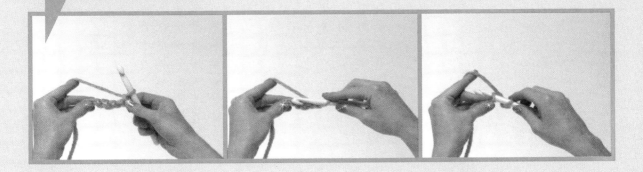

1. Starting with your foundation chain and a loop on your hook, hold your chain taut with your left hand and put your hook through the second chain stitch.

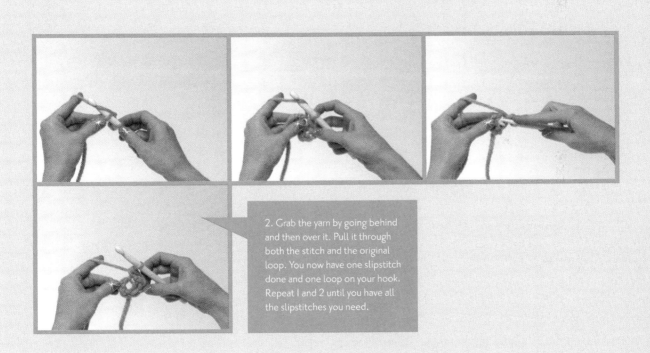

2. Grab the yarn by going behind and then over it. Pull it through both the stitch and the original loop. You now have one slipstitch done and one loop on your hook. Repeat 1 and 2 until you have all the slipstitches you need.

Slipstitch: The slipstitch is the smallest crochet stitch and is usually used to join rounds when you're crocheting a circle.

1. Insert hook in stitch. Yarn over hook.

2. Pull yarn through stitch.

3. Yarn over hook. Pull yarn through two loops on hook. Now you have one single crochet stitch.

Single crochet: This is the first "real" stitch used to make fabric. It creates the densest crochet and is used in diverse projects including three dimensional sculptures and toys.

4. Insert the hook through the next stitch and yarn over the hook. Pull the loop through, making two loops on your hook.

5. Yarn over again and pull through both loops. This is your second stitch. Repeat 4 and 5.

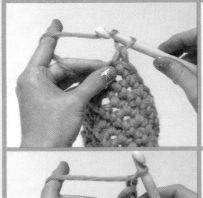

6. To start another row after the first is done, make a single chain stitch, called a "turning chain," then turn your work use your turning chain as the first stitch of the row, then continue in single crochet.

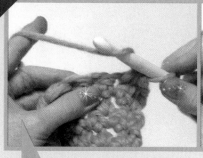

1. Starting with your foundation chain and a loop on your hook, wrap yarn around the hook.

2. Push the hook through the third chain, grab the yarn as before and pull through the stitch.

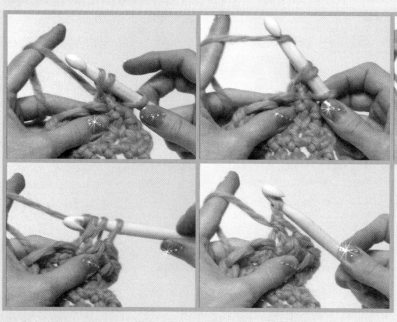

3. Now you have three loops on your hook. Grab yarn as above and pull it through the all three loops. Now you have a half double crochet and one loop on your hook.

4. Repeat steps 1 through 3, substituting "the next chain" for "the third chain" in step 2. To start another row after the first is done, make two chain stitches for the "turning chain," as the first stitch of the new row.

Half double crochet: Half double crochet creates a lighter and more flexible fabric than single. Just remember to wrap before you dip with this one.

DOUBLE CROCHET

A double crochet is a longer, more open and even more flexible stitch. It is made almost the same way as a half double crochet except that you will work the first stitch in the fourth chain. Follow the directions for a half double crochet except in step 3 you will pull the yarn through two loops on the hook. Then wrap the yarn around the hook again and pull through the remaining two loops to finish your stitch. To work the next row, chain 3 stitches for your "turning chain."

Hook Conversion Chart

METRIC	CROCHET USA	CROCHET UK
2		
2.25	B-1	13
2.75	C-2	12
3		
3.25	D-3	10
3.5	E-4	
3.75	F-5	9
4	G-6	
4.5	7	7
5	H-8	6
5.5	I-9	5
6	J-10	
6.5	K-10.5	
7		
8	L-11	
9	M-13	
10	N-15	
11.5	P-16	
12.75		
15		
16	Q	
19	S	
25		

Flower Brooch

You'll Need:

Worsted weight wool yarn (any color), you need only a fraction of a ball, a few yards at most

Size G (4 mm) crochet hook

3" square of decorative fabric for leaves

3" square of iron-on interfacing

Felt circle, 2" in diameter

Bar pin back (available at craft stores)

Iron

Washing machine

Needle and thread (basic sewing needle #7 and sewing thread)

3 rhinestones (optional)

Gem glue (optional)

BY DESIREE HAIGH

The idea of a flower pin was born in the fall of 2003. The flower phenom had hit, and after seeing artificial flower after artificial flower, I wanted to make one myself. My idea was to create something cozy yet beautiful, something fun but different. My yarn obsession came into play, and with a few rhinestones and some vintage fabric… voilá, a flower brooch. I have been making them ever since. I asked a fellow felted flower maker if the craze would ever end—she assured me that everyone will always want a pretty flower.

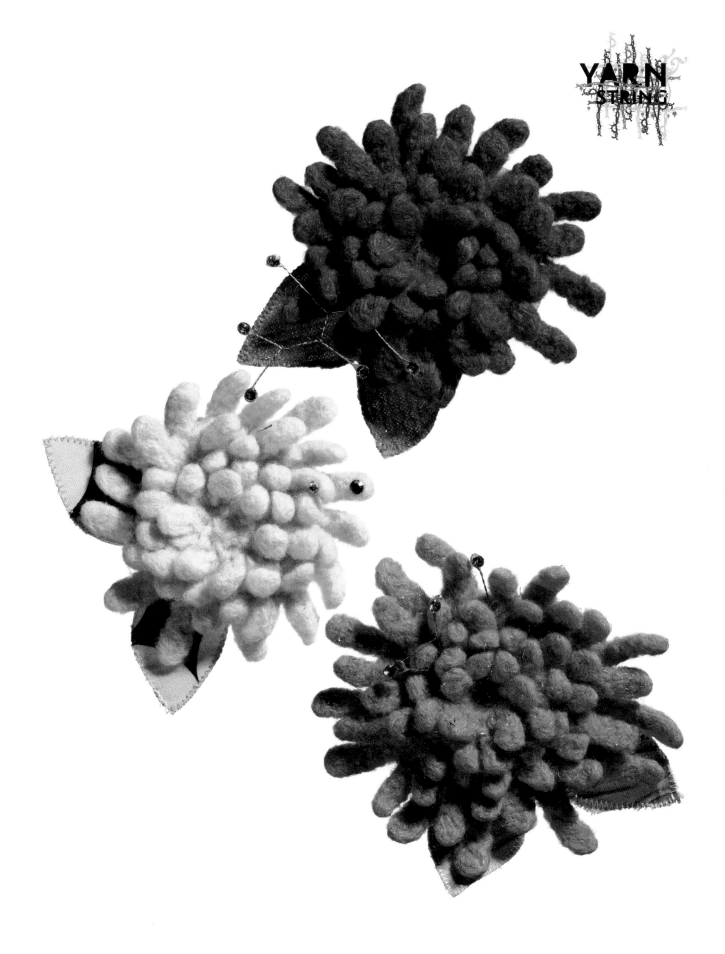

Unfelted flower

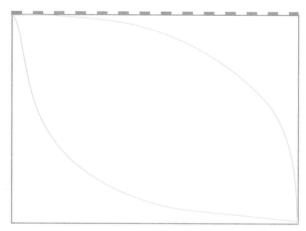

Leaf pattern, actual size. Dotted line indicates folded edge of fabric.

MAKING IT

1. Crochet flower (remember that you are felting this piece, so stitches need to be loose). Working the center of the flower first, chain 5, slip stitch in first chain to join into a ring.

Round 1: Single crochet 8 stitches in ring, slip stitch to first single crochet to join.

Round 2: (Chain 4, slip stitch in the second chain from the hook, slip in the next 2 chains, chain 1, slip stitch in the next single crochet—this will make one petal), repeat to make 8 petals. Join to the bottom of the beginning petal with a slip stitch.

Round 3: (Make a petal in the first chain 1 space in the previous round, chain 2) repeat 7 more times to make a second round of 8 petals with 2 chains in between each petal. Join to the bottom of the beginning petal with a slip stitch.

Round 4: Slip st to the first chain 2 space on the previous round, (chain 5, slip stitch in the second chain from the hook, slip in the next 3 chains, to make a longer petal), chain 1, slip stitch in the same chain 2 space, make another longer petal in the same chain 2 space, chain 1, slip stitch in the next chain 2 space. Repeat around to make 16 petals. Add more petals in each chain 2 space for a fuller flower. Join to the beginning petal with a slip stitch. Fasten off, leaving a 2" tail.

2. To felt your flower, throw it in the washing machine with jeans or towels. Use hot water and the proper amount of detergent for a load. Depending on your machine, you may need to wash flower twice.

3. Once your flower is felted enough to your liking, lay it on a flat surface covered with a towel. Shape and let fully dry.

4. Meanwhile, make leaves. Iron interfacing to the wrong side of the fabric. Fold square in half and cut through both layers to make two leaves.

5. To assemble pin, cut a strand of yarn and use to sew leaves to flower. Sew pin back to the center of the felt circle. Sew felt circle to flower.

If you have rhinestones this is the time to glue them on the petals. Enjoy your new brooch!

Hand Spun Yarn: Cherokee Hinrichs of Midnight and Lulu (TOP), Lexi Boeger of Plucky Fluff (MIDDLE), and Linda Scharf of Stone Leaf Moon (BOTTOM) all hand spin yarns of incredible beauty and richness in tiny batches.

Crochet Skull

BY DIANE BROMBERG

I had always thought I was more of a knitter than a crocheter simply because I never really liked the lacy look of crochet. But crochet is very appealing to the sculptor and builder in me. Knitting is like building with bricks, and crochet is like building with a fluid erector set—there are no bounds.

You'll Need:

1 ball Rowan Yarn, All Seasons Cotton, color natural

Size G (4 mm) crochet hook

Darning needle

White glue

Small paint brush

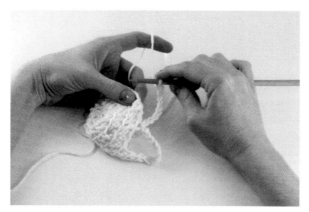

Attaching the eye.

Starting the nose.

I taught myself how to crochet out of an old book I bought at a flea market about five years ago: *America's Crochet Book* by Gertrude Taylor. There are no color pictures, no crazy fashion shots, nothing flashy. It is just a guide. I still haven't read it all but I use it as a reference when I need to learn how to create a new stitch.

When I was still learning basic stitches I kept myself entertained by making two-dimensional skulls. As I grew more comfortable I moved on to my first real piece: a spooky sexy bikini with a 2-D skull on each breast of the crochet top, glimpses of skin showing through the eye and nose holes.

I soon realized that I could make a skull in the round as well, and for a time I cranked those out. Eventually I felt compelled to blow it up—to make a giant crocheted skull. I used the same method I used for the small skulls but with a handmade giant crochet hook. The final product is about five feet tall and is so heavy I can barely lift it alone.

The size of my skulls are determined by the stitch I like to use to make the teeth. If I do a certain stitch for the tooth, how big would the rest of the skull have to be? In my experience a worsted weight yarn with a size G hook gives you a 3- to 4-inch tall skull. A finer sports or fingering weight ends up making a smaller skull.

To preserve and strengthen my skulls I use a brand of white glue, called Sobo, that dries flexible, not brittle. The glue should be watered down—start off with 1 tablespoon glue and 1/4 cup water. It should feel just a bit sticky and tacky when you rub your fingers together.

If you're just learning to crochet, and you want to get as far away as possible from grandma-style afghans, skulls are the way to go. Making skulls can teach you not only about basic stitches, but about the sculptural nature and possibilities of crochet—once you've grasped the concept the possibilities are endless.

If you know how to crochet, look at some images of a skull from different angles, think about its shape and just wing it. See what you make. My way is not the only way. Yours might come out crazy, but everyone needs a crazy spooky little skull to brighten their day.

MAKING IT

1. Start at the top of the head and work in spiral (think skull cap). Always work into back of loop.

Row 1: Chain 2, join chain with single crochet, 3 single crochet in same space. Work 2 single crochets into the next single crochet and 1 single crochet into the next single crochet.

Row 2: Continue around skull cap working 2 single crochets in each single crochet.

Row 3: Single crochet around increasing 1 single crochet in every other stitch (You should have 18 stitches).

Row 4: Crochet in half double crochet increasing 1 half double crochet into each third stitch to create a dome shape. (At this point there should be a total of 24 stitches.) Place marker (or contrast yarn) in next stitch to mark the center back of the head.

Row 5: Work 1 half double crochet into next 8 stitches, 2 half double crochets into next stitch (this

Double crochet around.

Attaching the jaw.

is the temple), 1 half double crochet into next 6 stitches, 2 half double crochets into next stitch (other temple), 1 half double crochet into next 8 stitches.
Row 6: Work 2 half double crochets into marked stitch, 1 double crochet into next 10 stitches.

2. EYES
Chain 9, slip stitch into 3rd stitch on the front of the skull, turn and slip stitch into last chain, turn, chain 9, slip stitch into 3rd stitch, 1 double crochet into next stitch and repeat around entire skull until 1 stitch before eye chain, slip stitch into 3rd chain, slip stitch into next 2 chain.

3. NOSE
Chain 7, slip stitch into 5th chain on next eye, slip stitch into next 2 chains, skip first double crochet after eye chain, double crochet into next 4 stitches, skip 1 stitch, (Check to see that eyes and nose have the right proportions), double crochet into next 4 stitches, skip 1 double crochet, double crochet into next 4 stitches, skip 1 stitch and slip stitch into next stitch, slip stitch across each stitch of nose chain, skip first stitch on eye, sl stitch into next stitch, half double crochet into next 5 stitches, skip 1 double crochet, half double crochet into next 3 stitches, skip 1 stitch, double crochet into 5 stitches, skip 1 stitch, slip stitch into next two slip stitches.

4. TOP TEETH
Chain 3 and slip stitch back into first stitch of this chain, skip 1 stitch, slip stitch in next 2 stitches, chain 3 and slip stitch into first stitch of this chain,

slip stitch in next 2 stitches, chain 3 and slip stitch into first stitch of this chain (3 teeth), skip stitch, single crochet into next 4 stitches, skip 1 stitch, single crochet into next 4 stitches, skip 1 stitch, single crochet into next 4 stitches.

5. JAW AND BOTTOM TEETH
You should now be 1 stitch from first upper tooth. Chain 20, slip stitch into 2nd single crochet after the last upper tooth. Turn, going back toward upper teeth, skip 1 stitch and single crochet into stitch between jaw chain and tooth, single crochet into next 4 chains on jaw, skip 2 chains, single crochet into next 2 chains, chain 3 and slip stitch into first stitch of this chain, single crochet into next 2 chains of jaw, chain 3 and slip stitch into first stitch of this chain, single crochet into next 2 chains of jaw, skip 2 chains, single crochet into next 4 chains of jaw, skip 2 chains, slip stitch into stitch at base of jaw between jaw chain and top tooth.

6. Fasten off with 6" of extra yarn. With a darning needle, weave end through back of work to bottom center of nose. Loosely (so as not to distort shape of nose cavity) pass needle straight up between eyes, knot and tuck end.

7. Stuff the skull with bits of paper towel into the shape you like. Using a paint brush, coat it with some watered down glue. Once the skull is dry, pull out stuffing and enjoy your unique object of desire.

The Blankie

You'll Need:

A lot of yarn. I used 12 balls of Rowan Cotton Tape in five colors: lap, sullen, electric, string, and bleached. At least three colors or textures will make a more visually interesting blankie. I like cotton yarn for babies, since it's washable and not scratchy. I used about a pound of yarn for a finished piece roughly 18" x 24". Each circle is about 8" on average. Pick fat yarn if you want it to go fast.

A crochet hook in a size that works for your yarn. With Cotton Tape, a size N (9 mm) should create a decent gauge. Too tight, use a bigger hook. Too loose, ratchet down.

Scissors

Tapestry needle or yarn needle

Standard quilting T-pins, towels, spray bottle for blocking

BY CALLIE JANOFF

When my best friend got knocked up, I knew I wanted to be the one to make the baby blanket. You know, THE BLANKIE, the one you love so much during childhood you take it with you to college and hide it under your pillow so your roommate won't see it. I also knew that no ordinary blanket—indeed, no blanket made from a pattern—would do. So I dug deep into my Northern California hippie roots and got inspired by some of the don't-box-me-in creativity I found in my photo albums and out-of-print '70s crochet books. (This technique is just as good for a throw if you have no upcoming babies. Even grown ups need blankies—they just call them something different.)

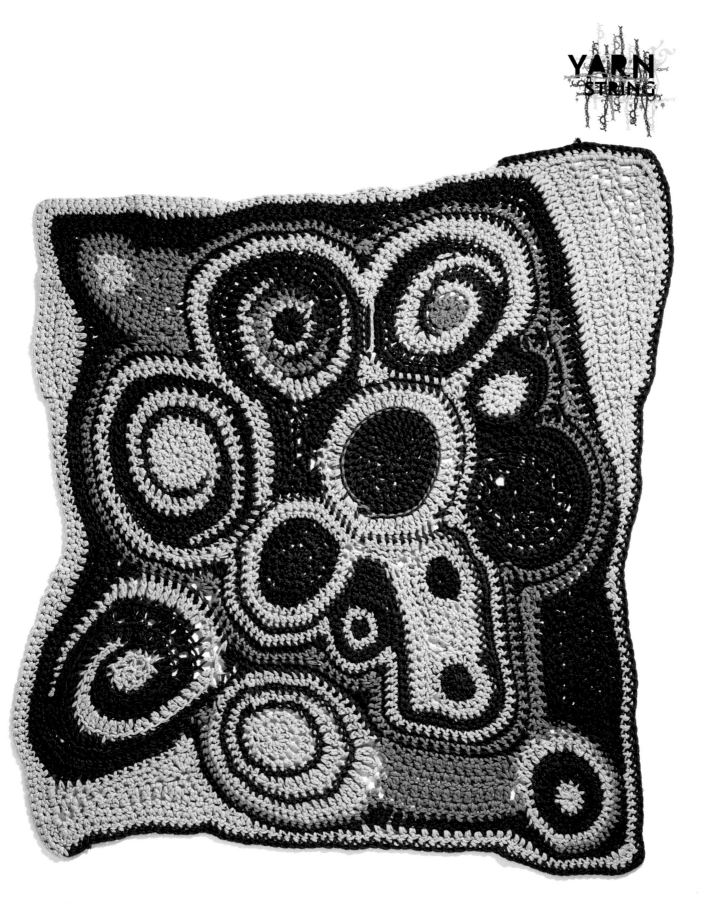

Multi-spirals

Making a gift for the baby was challenging, since it was hard to picture what she would be like. Would she look cute all wrapped up in khaki? Would her fingers like the feel of this or that yarn? There was no way to know, so there was no wrong way to make this project.

As for the pattern choice, circles make me happy: irregular circles in a free-form field of crochet make me really happy. What follows is not a pattern. It is a series of guidelines, ideas, and techniques to make your blankie. It will be pretty simple for an experienced crocheter, and a little challenging for a beginner. If crocheting is new for you, review your basic stitches and working in rounds first. (See Craftshop on page 39.) Start with easy regular circles and work your way up to the weird ones as you get more comfortable. And most importantly, relax and let stuff happen. Don't feel like everything has to be perfect or uniform: the beauty of the blankie is in the personality your own quirks give it. Don't squelch your flubs and hiccups: embrace them and incorporate them. After all, if you wanted a flawless blankie, you could pick one up at a department store.

MAKING IT

Begin by crocheting a bunch of circles—the more varied in size, uniformity, color, texture, and stitches the better. Here are several kinds of circles to make:

REGULAR ROUNDS

1. Make a slipknot that adjusts with the tail end.

2. Make a turning chain whose length corresponds to the height of your desired stitches—chain 1 for single crochet, chain 2 for half double crochet, chain 3 for double crochet, etc.

3. Crochet approximately 5 to 12 stitches into your initial adjustable loop—enough to go all the way around in a flat circle.

4. Use a slip stitch to join your last stitch to the top loop of your initial turning chain. You can choose to change colors or yarns here, or to continue with the same color.

5. Make another turning chain and crochet around your circle, increasing the circumference enough to keep your circle flat, but not so much that it becomes floppy or wavy. To increase, crochet two stitches into the same spot.

Regular rounds

6. Continue making rounds until you like the size of your circle. Fasten off when you're done.

REGULAR SPIRALS

1. Begin by making a chain 3 to 7 stitches long.

2. Use a slip stitch to attach the first chain to the last chain to form a loop.

3. Make a turning chain whose length corresponds to the height of your desired stitches—chain 1 for single crochet, chain 2 for half double crochet, chain 3 for double crochet, etc.

4. Crochet into each of your initial chains twice, increasing all the way around so that your circle lies flat.

5. Once you get all the way around, continue working into each stitch without stopping to make turning chains or slip stitching to close rounds, adjusting the number of increases you make to keep your circle flat. The further you get from the center, the less you will need to increase.

IRREGULAR CIRCLES

In the two examples above the goal is to make symmetrical shapes. The principle of making irregular shapes, on the other hand, is that each new round or ring of the circle consists of stitches of differ-

ing heights. The only new consideration for these oddballs is to remember that when increasing for a flat circle, the height of the different stitches plays a part. For instance, rounds worked in single crochet will not need to be increased as frequently as rounds in double or triple crochet. Below is an example of a way to achieve irregularity. Use this as a guide: it is more fun to make up your own circles.

1. Make a slipknot that adjusts with the tail end.

2. Chain 3 for your turning chain (this will count as your first double crochet—don't forget to crochet into it on your next round!).

3. Make 11 double crochets into your initial adjustable loop. Use a slip stitch to join your last stitch to the third loop of your initial turning chain.

4. Chain 1, make 2 single crochets into each of the next 2 stitches, then two half double crochets into each of the next two stitches, make two double crochets into each of the next four stitches, then two half double crochets into each of the next two stitches, make two single crochets into each of the next two stitches. Use a slip stitch to join your last stitch to your first stitch. You should have 24 stitches of varying heights. It should look vaguely egg-shaped.

You can continue to make as many rounds in as many colors as you like, building up to taller stitches in one part of your circle or another while you continue to increase to keep your circle flat. You can use the same principle when you are working in a spiral, changing colors or yarns whenever you feel like it.

MULTI-SPIRALS

1. Make a slipknot that adjusts with the tail end.

2. Chain 3 for your turning chain (this will count as your first double crochet—don't forget to crochet into it on your next round!).

3. Make 11 double crochets into your initial adjustable loop. Use a slip stitch to join your last stitch to the third loop of your initial turning chain.

4. Chain 3, double crochet twice into each stitch all the way around.

5. At the end of the round, don't close it; instead, make 3 half double crochets in the next 2 stitches. Pull the last loop of your stitch out long so it doesn't come undone and take your hook out of the loop.

6. Grab a new color or yarn and join to the next stitch.

7. Make single crochets in the next 3 stitches and 2 single crochets in the next stitch. Repeat.

8. Make half double crochets in the next 3 stitches and 2 half double crochets in the next stitch. Repeat.

9. Pull the last loop of your stitch out long so it doesn't come undone and take your hook out of the loop, and insert your hook back into your first yarn loop you left behind before.

10. Make single crochets in the next 3 stitches and 2 single crochets in the next stitch. Repeat.

11. Make half double crochets in the next 3 stitches and 2 half double crochets in the next stitch. Repeat. You can add third and fourth colors and yarns in the same way, repeating the process with each color or yarn as you come to the drawn-out loops.

PUT IT ALL TOGETHER

1. Make enough circles or other shapes to fill in most of your desired size and shape of baby blankie. It might help to cut out a piece of paper or fabric as a pattern to lay your pieces out on. This is the part where specific directions are hard to give, and your own inspiration and creativity comes in.

2. Join the circles to each other with a combination of tendrils and organic shapes and continue to fill in the background in a free-form, intuitive way. A tendril is a chain of any number of stitches that joins to your shapes with a slip stitch, a single crochet or a double crochet. An organic shape is a shape to fill in between the circles that isn't exactly a square or circle. Perhaps a trapezoid. Use different colors and yarns, work back and forth or around your shapes, and incorporate new shapes with slip stitches or chains. This is the moment to suspend your self-criticism and doubt and just try stuff. Don't be afraid to rip it out if you don't like it.

3. When all or most of your pieces are incorporated, you can work on making the outer rounds and rows conform to the shape of your pattern. Make corners by working back and forth with one of your organic fill-in shapes or by crocheting three stitches into a single stitch and, rotating the blankie to work along an adjacent side, continue around the edges.

4. Finish up with a round or two all the way around, working corners if you have them. Weave in all your ends with a tapestry needle.

BLOCK

1. Lay out your gorgeous blankie on a towel (or towels if you made a big blankie) and use big T-pins to anchor it and conform it to the shape of your pattern.

2. Spray the whole business down with plain water in a spray bottle. Let it dry completely overnight.

Crocheted Snow: When I see Abigail Doan's crochet, I think it's the Blair Good Witch Project. She crocheted this snow out of tencel, but she also works with found materials. such as twigs, weaving them into something sublime.

Bag o' Bags

BY DIANE BROMBERG

My friend Scott and I found a bag made of plastic bags at the harbor store on Fire Island. There was no tag or any information about who created them, but since they were fabulous (and inexpensive) we bought them all—all two of them. I loved the idea—how crafty! How eco!—and I loved the bags themselves so much that I had to make my own. The project turned out to be fairly labor intensive, but very, very satisfying. And the bags are beautiful as well as functional.

You'll Need:

Sharp scissors

Size K (6.5 mm) crochet hook

30-40 lightweight plastic grocery bags from a supermarket

3 medium size, heavier weight bags, from a bookstore or clothing store, for example

Gauge = Bottom/heavier bags = 7 stitches/5 rows = 4" in double crochet

Body/grocery bags = 9 stitches/8 rows = 4" in double crochet

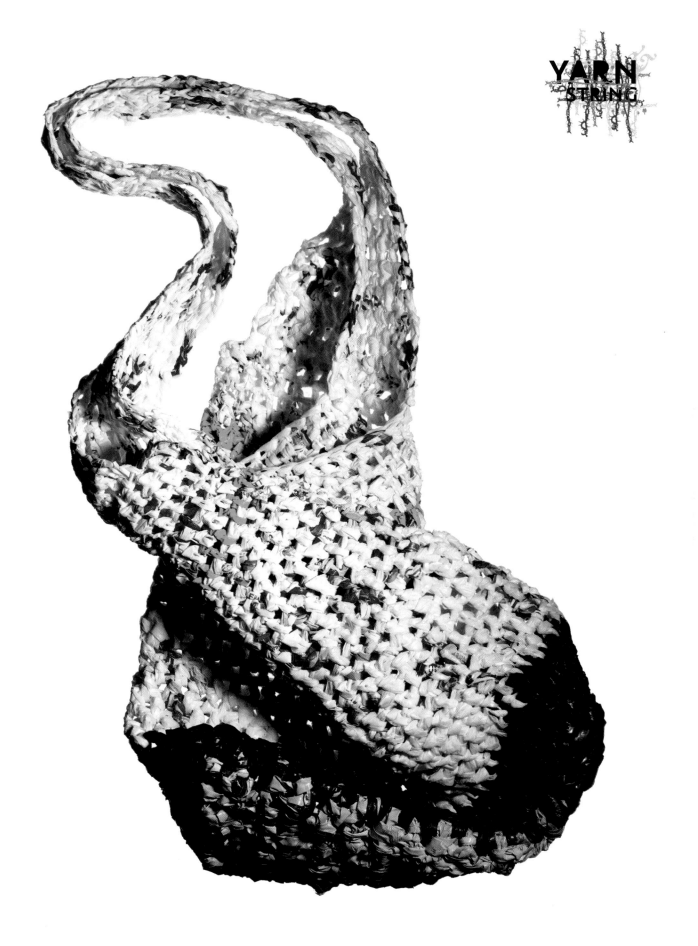

YARN
STRING

I worry about our environment, and find that the more I can recycle, the more hopeful I feel. The bag of bags is the perfect project to undertake if you can never find enough things to do with your plastic bags. Essentially you are spinning your own yarn out of refuse, and it's one of the best acts of recycling that you can do. Using bags that are all the same will make your bag more uniform, you can achieve more of a crazy quilt look by using bags of different colors.

MAKING IT

1. Cut bags into strips approximately 1/2" wide. Try to keep the strips approximately the same width, but don't worry too much if they vary a little. (See diagram for how to cut the bags in a spiral to maximize the length of your yarn.)

2. Wind the bag strips into balls.

3. Crochet the bottom of the bag using the "yarn" made from the heavier bags. Keep all stitches loose and your yarn ends tucked as you go. If bags are sticking on needle, use hand lotion for lube.

4. BOTTOM OF THE BAG

Chain 12.
Row 1: Double crochet in 4th chain from hook and continue in each chain across row, chain 3, turn. You should have 9 stitches.
Row 2: Double crochet into spaces between stitches (rather than into stitches) across row, chain 3, turn.
Row 3: Repeat row 2 until piece measures 11". You'll have a 5" x 11" rectangle.

5. SIDES OF THE BAG

Round 1: After you've finished the bottom of the bag, instead of turning work, continue along long edge of rectangle (using lighter strips), one stitch into each space between rows and one stitch into each space between stitches all the way around the four sides of your rectangle. Continue working in rounds around and up the sides of your bag until it measures 12" high. Fasten off.

6. CROCHET THE STRAPS

Lay bag flat.
Row 1: Starting 1" from outside edge, double crochet 9 stitches in towards center, chain 3, turn.
Row 2: Repeat row 1.
Row 3: Repeat row 1, but decrease at end of row by working last 2 stitches together. Repeat row 3 until 4 double crochets and 1 turning chain remain. Repeat this row until strap measures 20".
Next Row: Increase one stitch at the beginning of row. Repeat last row until you have 9 stitches and 1 turning chain.
Joining Row: Slip stitch strap to side of bag beginning 1" from outside edge. Fasten off.
Make two straps.

CRAFT MORE

Other things to crochet (or even knit) with plastic bag yarn:
✤ Door mats
✤ Bath mats
✤ Placemats
✤ Carmats
✤ Drainage for plants
✤ Fruit bowls
✤ Braided rugs (braid with the plastic, then sew/tie together)

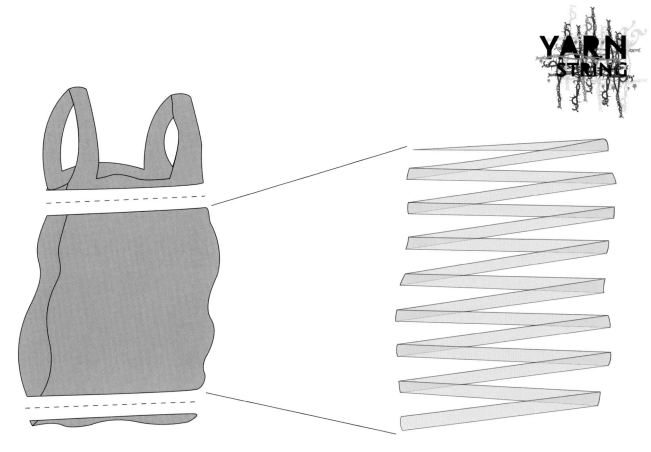

Cut a plastic bag in a spiral pattern.

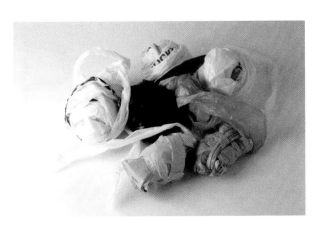

OTHER THINGS TO DO WITH PLASTIC BAGS

✤ Re-use as shopping bags—some stores even give you a small discount if you bring your own bags.

✤ Use as liners for small garbage cans.

✤ Keep a stash in the car for collecting trash.

✤ Take on walks for impromptu berry picking or shell collecting.

✤ Donate: to thrift stores, soup kitchens, food banks, local day care centers or schools, local libraries, etc.

✤ Use to cover your bike seat if it gets wet (or to keep it dry).

✤ Take your lunch to work in them.

✤ Use in place of plastic wrap (you'd be surprised how often you don't need a new piece of flat plastic wrap).

✤ Use them to bring home your sweaty gym clothing.

✤ Store small craft projects that you aren't going to be working on immediately.

✤ Use as disposable gloves (i.e. when checking your oil, taking out leaky garbage, or pulling up poison ivy).

✤ Stuff pillows (can be a little crinkly sounding, but in general a great substitute for foam bits).

✤ Poop scoopering.

✤ Tape together to use as a mini-tarp or to cover a table during messy crafts.

✤ Tie to a big stick to use as a scarecrow.

✤ For travel: keep a stash in your suitcase—great for wrapping up wet toiletries, for keeping souvenirs separate, and for blocking up mouse holes in dodgy hotels.

Knit Hammock

BY ANNIKA GINSBERG

One summer I found myself doing something I never imagined myself doing: knitting a hammock. Although the actual knitting skills of this project are fairly basic, be warned that the large needle size and the material can make this project challenging. I found that after a few rows of knitting, the hammock and I found our rhythm together. Knitting a hammock will make you feel like you have the ability to provide yourself with a comfy place to sleep at night should you ever be stranded on a desert island. I still marvel at how beautiful and sea-like this creature is that I created.

You'll Need:

14 balls of American Hemp twine 20 lb (approximately 3,800 feet) in your choice of colors

Utility knife (Exacto or other brand)

1/2" diameter dowel, 36" long

Sandpaper (fine and very fine grit)

1 sheet of wax paper

Rubber bands

A tennis ball

2 3" diameter jump rings (optional)

2 S-hooks (optional)

MAKING IT

1. Cut dowel in half to make two knitting needles.

2. On one end of each needle, cut a point with a utility knife. Sand the pointed ends with fine grit sandpaper, then move to a very fine grit. Rub a piece of wax paper over the entire needle to prevent snags.

3. Cut a tennis ball in half with utility knife. Cut a 1" X in the top of each half of the ball. Insert the needle into the X so that the fuzzy side is facing the needle point as a stopper for needle end.

4. Cast on 100 stitches holding two strands of hemp twine together.

5. Knit every row (garter stitch) until the piece measures 6 1/2' or about 80 rows. Keep your stitches nice and loose so the hammock is stretchy. (Secure the tips of the needles together with a rubber band when you are not working on the project.) My hammock is in free form stripes of blue, white, and red.

6. Measure the hammock. Stretch it a bit vertically. It should be about 7' long. If too short, keep knitting. If too long, unravel until right length.

7. Bind off loosely.

8. Weave in the ends 10 stitches horizontally and then go back across row to the edge. Tie off securely.

9. Cut 50 pieces of twine each 2 1/2 to 3 yards long. The exact length is not as important as that all the pieces are the same length.

10. Lay the hammock on the floor. Beginning at one end, work left to right with the first end stitch. Weave one of your twine lengths in and out of 2 to 4 stitches through the posts of the stitch. Pull both ends of the twine through so that the ends of the piece are even. You can place a paperweight, heavy book, or rock on top of the ends to keep them straight and somewhat taut while you weave the next twine length. Repeat until you are at the last stitch (25 lengths of twine per side.)

11. Bring all pieces of twine together and pull them taut to make sure each will take an even load of weight when the hammock is hung. You may want a friend to help you with this.

12. Twist the ends together and tie into a figure 8 loop knot or a tassel knot. With figure 8 loop knot, you can take an additional piece of twine and wind it around all the strands in your loop to make it look neater and be less likely to tangle. An alternate method is to attach your pieces of twine with a hitching or lark's head knot to your jump or hammock rings. You can then weave each end of each piece through and around the post between 2 stitches and tie off with a figure 8, Flemish or Savoy knot.

13. Find a nice spot with two trees. Wind rope around each tree and connect rope to S-hooks. Connect jump rings to S hooks. Adjust as needed. Tie up your ropes.

CRAFT MORE

✤ You might knit with a lightweight boat rope or laundry line cotton instead of the hemp twine. Remember that if you want your hammock to live outside, it needs to be made out of a material that can get wet without rotting or getting moldy.

Figure 8 loop knot

Half-covered knot

Final knot

FABRIC & THREAD

part 2

Bedazzled Table Linens

BY KIRSTEN HUDSON

I've always loved cloth napkins. Not only are they more eco-friendly, they make the table look great. Placemats protect the table like a tablecloth does, but they are less fussy, and they allow you more flexibility with how you dress up your table. If you love rhinestones—the downtown word for crystals, which sounds a lot swankier—but really can't bear to see another bedazzled jacket, T-shirt or totebag, this is your chance to indulge in a whole other genre. These napkins and placemats are easy to make, unique and special. I came up with this project because my decades old linen napkins were starting to get a little tatty. The first one turned out so nicely, however, that I made the project into a wedding present (which was received really well).

You'll Need:

2 yards of fabric (for 4 napkins and 4 placemats)

12-24 flat-backed crystals (a.k.a. rhinestones) and backs (with short prongs) per napkin/ placemat—more or less to taste. I used the ss20 size.

Glue or stud setter

Sewing scissors

For fabric, I recommend linen, with a rough weave (the more visible the weave the better I think), but if you have cotton, hemp, or heavy silk, that would work well too. I stick with an earthy palette—natural, olive green, dark brown, earthy yellow—because these colors provide contrast for the crystal sparkle. For the most part, solid fabrics work better than those with patterns, but if you have some great patterned cotton or linen, by all means give it a try. Placemats should be made out of heavier fabric than napkins, but they don't have to be entirely stiff. Your placemats and napkins also don't have to match exactly. In fact, you might want to make two different sets of napkins and tablecloths, which could look good together.

The quality and cost of crystals varies considerably. Swarovski crystals are of reliably good quality (and come in some amazing colors), but they can be expensive. If you can, bring your fabric to a store that carries a selection of crystals so that you can lay the crystal down on the fabric and see how it is going to look. Try vaguely matching (i.e. olive green crystals on olive green linen) as well as contrast (pinky-purply crystals on olive green fabric). I also prefer larger crystals to smaller ones.

MAKING IT

1. Wash the fabric. Nobody wants to dry clean their napkins, so it's important that you be able to throw them in the wash. Washing the fabric before you start will make sure that enough shrinkage has taken place so as not to affect post decoration washing.

2. Cut or rip the fabric. Napkins can be anywhere from 10" x 10" to 16" x 16". I like them on the big side. Placemats are typically about 14" x 18", but you could also make them a little smaller if you needed to use less fabric or if you have a little table or if you have a big table and want to sit lots of people around it. I like the look of raw ripped edges, but some fabric doesn't rip well, so you may need to use scissors. Save the scraps!

3. Once you have a set of napkins and/or placemats that are about the right size, start affixing crystals according to your chosen method. You can use a special glue (i.e. Gem-Tac), but I prefer to set the crystals with metal prong backs. (Long prongs are more secure, but short prongs look better. I recommend short prongs—if a crystal falls off you can always replace it.) You use an inexpensive tool called a rhinestone or stud setter. The Bedazzler brand version is readily available, but the stripped down generic version is cheaper and easier to use. There is also a tool called a Bejeweler, which automates gluing if you like the look of glue but tend to get it all over.

You can plan where you want the crystals to go, or you can just start with one, then affix the next in another area, then another in another area, etc. I prefer the latter approach. Hold up the napkin or placemat after you put down each crystal,

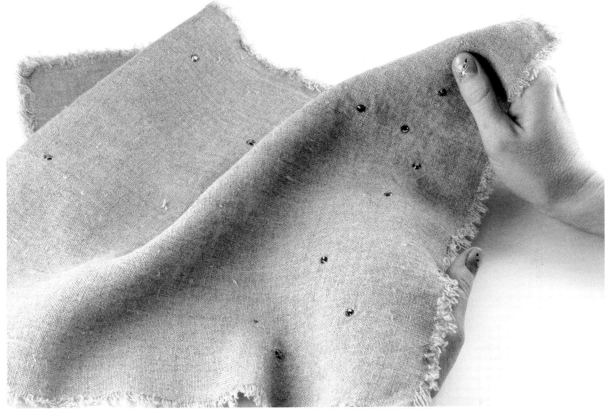

You can place crystals in any pattern you choose.

and choose a spot for the next. Space them out and don't use too many. Maybe put down six or seven on each napkin and then take a look and add more if you think it needs it. You can also fold up the napkins to see how they are going to look folded. I used between 12-14 rhinestones on each napkin and placemat.

4. Finish the edges. I like to leave the edges of the napkins raw, but if the raw edge isn't doing it for you, you have a number of options. If you know how, you can sew a traditional hem, which will make your table linens look very polished and professional. Another great way to finish the linens is just to machine sew around and around near the edge. This will help stop the fabric from fraying,

and it also provides an organic looking decorative edge. As for thread color, you could match the fabric color or, better yet, you could do a coordinating match (dark brown thread on light brown napkins) or a contrast (magenta thread on yellow napkins).

5. Use the scraps to make napkin ties. You can just cut or rip a piece that is the right size and leave it at that, or you could decorate the ties as well.

6. Have company over and show off your beautifully dressed table.

Fanged Bleach Stencil Shirt

BY SUSAN BARBER

There are many ways to make a bleach stencil for fabric, and this one works pretty well. Eventually the bleach eats through the fabric and instead of lighter areas of design, you'll have holes. This can look cool, but it's good to keep in mind while designing your stencil—if the negative spaces are too big you'll just end up with huge holes in your shirt.

You'll Need:

A stencil you've made or use the one on page 76

8 1/2" x 11" piece of acetate (you can use plain paper, but acetate will make a longer lasting stencil)

1 sheet of Drytac TwinTac or other double faced adhesive sheet

Exacto knife and blades

T-shirt or sweatshirt

Cardboard (enough to fit inside of a shirt, 11" x 17" at most)

Butcher paper or wax paper

Packing tape

Rubber gloves

Spray bottle

Bleach

Iron

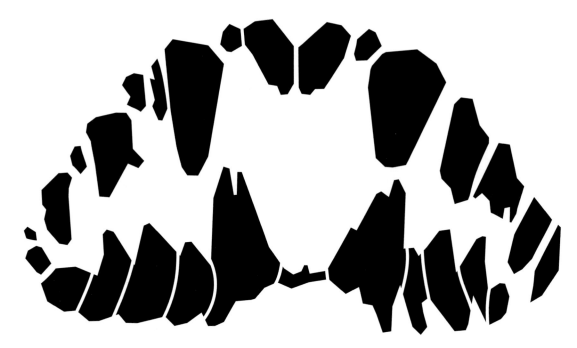

Enlarge stencil as needed.

I like to use a gray shirt, although any color will work, as long as it's cotton fabric. It just depends on the look you're going for. The results can be surprising: bleach on black makes a pinkish color, far from white. I recommend a tiny test on the inside hem with a bleach-soaked Q-tip to help predict the results. This is kind of a high-risk project, not good for your favorite eighty-dollar t-shirt, better for a thrifted or found item. Also, don't wash the finished piece more than necessary as that accelerates the deterioration of the already weakened fabric.

MAKING IT

1. Photocopy your stencil onto the acetate.

2. Adhere sheet of TwinTac to entire back of acetate.

3. Cut out your stencil with an Exacto knife.

4. Remove backing from TwinTac and adhere to shirt in desired location. Save backing.

5. Place cardboard inside shirt.

6. Make a mask around the stencil with butchers or wax paper and tape with packing tape in place to protect the rest of your shirt from bleach.

7. Wearing rubber gloves, fill spray bottle with bleach.

8. Spray bleach slowly over stencil. It will take awhile for the bleaching to occur. You don't want to use more than necessary to avoid making holes, but if you use too little your pattern will be blotchy.

9. Carefully remove mask and stencil from shirt. If you want to reuse your stencil, replace the backing on adhesive and set it in a safe place to dry (out of reach of children and animals, duh). Carefully throw away the bleach mask.

10. Without moving the iron too much, iron over your design on highest heat setting your fabric will allow. Setting this way helps whiten the bleach and keeps it from spreading.

11. Wash before wearing.

Stitch Sampler

Of all the Craftivity techniques, sewing is probably the most basic and widely used. Projects from T-shirt Undies and Moth Embroidered Sweater to Felted Pillows and Stuffed Octopus all call for some degree of stitchery.

Stitches (*from left to right, top to bottom*): herringbone, blanket, satin, chain, threaded back, back, split, running.

Moth Embroidered Sweater

You'll Need:

One or more moth-eaten sweaters. The simpler the sweater the better. You don't want your stylized moth holes competing with a pattern. Also, you want a fine knit like cashmere or merino. The technique doesn't work on chunky knits.

Thread in a contrasting color or colors, like pink for a brown sweater, fuchsia with orange or vibrant green on navy. You can also make each hole a different color, although I didn't because I didn't want it to seem too overpowering. I did have a lot of holes to fix after all. I use regular thread but you might try silk thread that would snag less.

A thin needle with a small eye (#7 needle). You don't want to make the hole bigger by using a thick needle with a big eye.

BY JENNIFER KABAT

Lemons into lemonade—there are all sorts of sayings about how you're supposed to transform bad things into good. So I've got a new one: moths and sweaters. In particular, cashmere sweaters. You know those moths that eat up your sweaters and have you swearing when autumn comes and you take out your favorite cardigan? Well, those moth holes are a good thing, I promise.

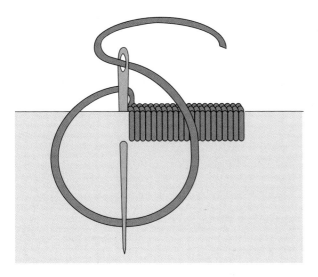

Buttonhole stitch
Begin by holding the thread along the cut or top edge of the fabric, with the needle pointing in the direction you want to sew. You will be working from the edge of the fabric down. Bring needle point through the fabric from the wrong side about 1/16"-1/8", or the length of your buttonhole stitch, down from the edge to left. Now push the needle point through the fabric to the right side, loop the thread around the tip of the needle point clockwise. Hold eye of needle in place with your thimble while you form the knot by letting go of thread and pulling needle through loop and the fabric. Pull thread near knot to tug it onto edge of fabric. Make next stitch next to it and closer to you.

I live in a particularly moth-stricken section of London. At least, my dry cleaner says so. "We have an infestation of them," he'll sigh, and shake his head. They apparently like the damp climate, and I live on a particularly wet block with the River Effra flowing right under my house. (Oh, what I wish I'd known before I bought my house.) So now I've joined the ranks of "if you can't beat them" and learned to espouse my mother's ethos that something bad is actually good for the moral fiber. Or that when life gives you lemons…

I've spent years trying to repair the tiny holes moths have munched into my sweaters. I've perfected dainty little stitches designed to be invisible to the naked eye, but such a strategy wouldn't work with my gray V-neck sweater. I got it when I was a teen (20 years ago now, if you must know) and was recently close to throwing it out. There was no way to repair the decades of damage, so I decided to turn the bug into a benefit, and make a feature of the fact that my sweater was verging on Swiss cheese. I decided to play up my moth holes and outline them—also shoring them up in the process to stop further fraying—in bright red thread. Now, thanks to the moths, I have a sweater with an asymmetric red pattern across the front, and people stop me to ask where they can buy it.

Every time I wear mine, I get compliments on it, whether it's from hotshot Italian furniture designers, Dutch felt makers, people down at my local coffee shop, or kids at the door waiting to get in to

a gig. It's a good conversation starter, and since my holes are red, people always joke about bullets and wounds. Which gives me the opportunity to say in a very melodramatic voice, "Worse. It's moths…"

MAKING IT

1. Thread your needle and knot it so the thread is doubled. You'll use more thread initially, but it will save you time.

2. On the underside of the sweater, poke the needle through the wool and up around the edge of the moth hole, as if you were going to sew a buttonhole.

3. Outline the hole (and reinforce it) by using buttonhole stitch. Stitch around it, starting underneath, looping the threaded needle up and around the fraying edge of the hole and then down again just a fraction over from where you started.

4. To make the hole strong and stop all fraying, you'll want to circle around the hole like this two to three times until no more bits of frayed wool poke out. The hole will be reinforced and feel stiffer, and you will see a solid block of color outlining the moth hole and protecting your sweater.

5. Last of all: wear your sweater!

SHOWCASE

Felted Cashmere Blanket: Leslie Baum is a Chicago-based painter. She made this queen-sized block quilt, replete with hand-embroidered animals, from second hand cashmere sweaters.

Felting

BY SCOTT BODENNER

If your experience of felt is limited to kindergarten art projects, or if you think that felt is something that is sold by the square in craft stores, prepare to have your mind blown. Felting is a process, requiring only woolens and a washing machine, and once you get started, you too may become a felting devotee.

WHAT IS THIS STUFF YOU CALL FELT?

The primary colored easy-craft staple is one kind of felt. Another is an industrial material, used for insulation and other hard-core non-craft purposes. But the felt that crafting lifers are interested in is an evolution of knit fabrics.

Knit fabrics have the benefit of tremendous give and bias. Felting causes the yarn's fibers to mesh together so they maintain their properties, but will not unravel when cut. You can turn anything woolen (including cashmere and alpaca but not acrylic) into felt. So if you have multiple sweaters made by your grandmother who thinks you are 9 feet tall, or if you can't resist buying beautiful thrift store woolens no matter how badly they fit, or if you have a huge pile of knit test swatches, felting is the magical solution to your problems.

HOW IT WORKS

When you felt a knit fabric, the temperature changes and agitation causes the curly barbed wool fibers to straighten out and then spring back and lock together, so they get all tangled up. This means that you get a tighter, sturdier piece of fabric.

HOW TO DO IT

The easiest method of felting is to throw sweaters into a washing machine for a normal cycle (hot or warm wash, cold rinse). A small amount of soap (try 1/8 of what you might normally use) will also aid in felting. In the washing machine, hot water felts more than warm water. Similarly, a long cycle felts more than a short cycle.

CONTROLLING THE PROCESS

If sweaters aren't felted to your desired thickness or smallness, they may require multiple washings, but be careful. The first wash may not seem to do much. Then with the second wash your old XXXL fits your 8-year-old niece.

So, if you are shrinking a baggy sweater and it is close to what you'd like, stop before it gets way too small.

Arms often become too short during felting. One solution is to wrap them in a 3" wide strip of a non-wool material. Looping, and knotting each loop seems to work best since it won't come undone in the machine. This technique is similar to tie dying, so you could choose areas you want to pucker out and not felt, tie them off and throw that into the wash.

Felting gives you freedom because exposed edges won't unravel. You can tie them with loops of yarn, or crochet them together, or sew them with a machine or by hand. My favorite method involves a latch hook or knitting machine needle to create seams that have give like the knit.

The magic of felt is now your own mighty saber to wield at unruly wool-based fabrics. Shrink and re-shape away! Felted material can be cut and sewn into new garments, quilts, rugs, hats, potholders, toilet seat covers, anything requiring the durability, flexibility, density, and dangerous beauty of felt.

TIPS

✤ PATTERNS: A sweater with a graphic multicolor pattern may look bad from the front, but becomes lines of color on the back. These might fuzz together and become beautiful during felting.

✤ COLOR BLEEDING: Sweaters often bleed so make sure that you combine colors that will look good if they tint each other.

✤ SHRINKAGE: Shrinkage occurs more in the length than the width of a knit. Ribbing, at the bottom and sleeves of a sweater, tends to felt less and sewn seams often don't felt at all.

✤ Sweaters (or other pieces of knit fabric) of all wool or nearly all wool, alpaca and cashmere felts are dreamy. Your closet, your best friend's closet and thrift stores are all good resources.

✤ Make sure the sweaters don't matter too much to you since felting is something of a voodoo art, and there is always a chance of over-felting.

Felt Pillows

BY SCOTT BODENNER

Felting is a process that I loved as soon as I learned it. Felt is warm and dense and doesn't fray. I love cuddling up in a favorite sweater on a cold day, and with these pillows, you can cuddle up all through the cold months with a perfect palette of colors and textures of wool. You also have the added warmth of knowing you are recycling as well as making something beautiful.

MAKING IT

1. Gather sweaters that are no longer wearable.

2. Felt by throwing in the washing machine. See page 82 for felting instructions.

3. Repeat until you're happy with the texture.

4. Cut up the felted sweaters into any shapes you want, although squares are always good.

5. Sew pieces together in backstitch to make two 15" squares in whatever pattern makes you smile.

6. Sew three sides of the two squares together to make a pillow case.

7. Fill with down pillow stuffing. Sew fourth side in backstitch to close pillow.

CRAFT MORE

✤ Make a felt quilt by felting Fair Isle or cabled sweaters or wool blankets. Cut into squares. Crewel or embroider together.

✤ Use overcast stitch for your edges.

You'll Need:

4 sweaters (or other pieces of knit fabric) of all wool or nearly all wool. Pattern makes pillows approximately 15" x 15"

A washing machine

Down or down substitute pillow filling

Needle and thread

Scissors

Felted Necklace

BY NAD THITADILAKA

My fascination with felting began a couple of years ago, totally by accident. I put my knitted hat into the washing machine rather than send it to the dry cleaner. The result was that it shrunk into the size of a softball. From then on, I started throwing knitted fabric into the washer and experimenting with the results.

You'll Need:

For the cord, 2 balls any eyelash novelty yarn of about the same weight. I used one ball Habu Textiles A-28B Kasumi yarn, I ounce, 121 yards, and one ball Habu Textiles A-25 Cork Chenille yarn, I ounce, 99 yards. Or use any sport weight knitting yarn, preferably in something luxurious like silk. Remember this is going around your neck.

I pair size 3 (3.25 mm) knitting needles

I size 38 felting needle

1/4 pound wool roving. This will give you enough to play with.

Dish detergent

Rubber gloves if your hands are sensitive to detergent or wool

Wrap the roving into a ball.

Secure loose wool on roving ball with a felting needle.

Wet the roving ball to complete felting.

As I became more adept at felting, I started using some specialized techniques and materials. For this project, I needle and wet felt wool roving into a necklace. Wool roving is carded wool fibers—they have been combed and cleaned. You would also use roving to spin yarn. Felting needles are covered in tiny barbs. When you push the needle repeatedly through the roving, the barbs mix the fibers, locking them together. Then you wet the ball to finish the process. You should definitely try to make a few balls just to get the hang of it and see how the wool shrinks in the felting. Once you know the magic formula... the rest is cinchy.

MAKING IT

1. Cast on 5 stitches on the knitting needles using both yarns held together (A-25 and A-28B or any yarn of your choice) and knit in stockinette stitch until you reach the desired length for your necklace, about 29 1/2".

2. Sew the two ends of this strip together; it will curl in on itself to form a rounded cord.

3. Using your hand, try to separate the wool roving into a strip of wool. Carefully keep wrapping the wool roving strip around the seam of the necklace cord until it forms a ball 3" in diameter. The ball will be light and fluffy like cotton candy.

4. Use the felting needle to secure the loose wool onto the knitted seam, by slowly poking the needle through the wool area back and forth until the loose ball doesn't move and becomes denser.

It should now be well affixed to the necklace, fully covering the seam. By using a felt needle, you can create a dense ball quickly and when you wet the wool it becomes a solid ball.

5. Fill the bowl with hot water from your tap and a squirt of soap. If you use too much soap, it can retard the felting process.

6. Sprinkle hot soapy water on to the ball and start to shape it with your hand, as if you're making a meatball. Be gentle at first. Get the whole ball wet and keep your hand loosely cupped. Move the wet ball in your palm until it has shrunk to half its original size. Be careful not to put too much pressure on the ball at first or it may crease. Keep circling the ball in your hand until it hardens. This process takes about 5 to 7 minutes.

7. Rinse the ball thoroughly with cold water to remove all the excess soap. Pat with a towel and let air dry.

8. Wear it out, sing it loud, be proud of what you've made.

CRAFT MORE

✛ Make a bracelet or ring using the same technique.

✛ Make just the ball and use as a brooch.

T-Shirt Underwear

BY LOGAN BILLINGHAM

There once was a boxy, cropped tee bearing an airbrushed-style kitty face that had somehow appeared in my scrap pile. I liked the artwork, but the shape of the shirt was all wrong. Although I did not yet know why, I had to keep it around. Inspiration struck as I was sorting laundry. As I held up my favorite pair of undies, marveling at their hip-hugging shape, low waist, and full bottom, I realized the destiny of my kitty shirt. Armed with my best scissors, I went to work, and within a few hours I had brand new undies. The kitty face found a home on the back side, and there was plenty of material left for the front.

You'll Need:

One t-shirt: the thinner and softer the material, the better. Heavy duty tees will make bulky underwear.

Flat elastic cord, 1/4" or 1/8" wide, 48" or enough to go around both legs and your waist

6" x 4" additional very soft, thin cotton knit for crotch lining. It's best to use very thin material for this part to avoid bulky seams. You can use a piece of the t-shirt.

Sewing machine

Thread

Scissors

Straight pins

Piece of paper (2' x 4') or enlarged pattern printout

I know you've got them, lurking in drawers, the back of the closet, in the "giveaway" pile. Unwearable yet indispensable, flawed, misshapen, or just too small, there are some t-shirts you just can't part with. These shirts need not hide in the dark any longer. They can begin a new life—as underwear.

Find a t-shirt that strikes your fancy. I have used shirts with printed pictures or words, or abstract patterns—anything I thought would look good on a butt. If you're doing this for the first time and/or you are an unpredictable seamster, you might not want to use your prized material possession right away. One t-shirt should be enough material, but you can check to make sure, using the pattern. (You can turn the shirt sideways, as long as you don't mind the artwork going sideways too.)

Since t-shirt material varies greatly, sometimes my undies turn out tight and slim, sometimes they are more like bloomers, but I like them either way.

I just try to go with the flow, figure out what the fabric wants to do, and always, always make small adjustments as I go. Make everything bigger than you think it needs to be, and then make it 10% bigger than that! You can always make it smaller, but not the other way around.

It's true that this creation will usually be covered up and not many people will ever see what a wonderful thing you have made. But the lucky few who do will appreciate it all the more. This makes a good gift for a friend, especially if the shirt used is especially amusing or embarrassing. But good luck getting your friend's hip size without arousing suspicion.

MAKING IT

1. Take your hip measurement (the circumference at the widest point), divide by 2 and add 1". This distance should correspond to the width of the pattern, right across the middle (along a horizontal

T-shirt undies shown inside out with crotch piece sewn in.

line halfway down from the waist). If your material seems stretchier than a typical tee, make adjustments as you see fit. You can print out the pattern and enlarge it to the right size, or you can just eyeball it and copy the shape onto your own paper. I recommend using a paper pattern because then it's easier to repeat the project. Also, if you end up adjusting a proportion somewhere, you can annotate the pattern and have a record of your change. You may notice that the pattern looks bigger than the undies you normally wear. Do not worry.

2. Situate the pattern on top of the t-shirt so that the artwork is in the right place on the underwear. Pin the paper to the fabric before cutting, as t-shirt material tends curl once it's been cut.

3. Take your crotch piece and hem the wider end, folding the edge over either once or twice.

4. Lay the front main piece right side up on a flat surface. Over this lay the back piece, right side down, with the lower edge lining up with the piece underneath. Don't worry if it doesn't look like the sides line up properly. Just make sure the lower edge is right.

5. Place the crotch piece wrong side up directly on top of the other two pieces, and line up the bottom edge of that as well.

6. Pin the three layers together along this lower edge, and then sew through them all. Leave a 1/4"-seam allowance. Double stitch or do a fine stitch length.

7. Lay the whole thing flat as before but this time line up the side edges of the front and back main pieces. Pin the sides, and then double stitch, leaving a 1/2"-seam allowance.

8. Hold up the undies by the waist so the front is facing you, and let the crotch piece hang straight down. Lay the garment on your work surface, letting the crotch piece remain pointing downward. Take the crotch and fold it around to the front, so that it lines up nicely with the front section's edges, and pin it in place. The bottom seam's raw edge should be covered up now, and the right side of the

crotch piece should be facing you. At this point you should have something closely resembling a pair of inside-out undies with some pins in the crotch. Nice, eh?

9. Now would be a good time to try on the underwear, if it's for you. Keep it inside out and watch out for those pins. At this point the undies should be snug at the hips, but it's ok if they are loose around the leg holes and the waist. If the hips are not snug, take in the hip seams a bit (taking care to snip the excess fabric on the inside of the running seam back to 1/2" if necessary).

START WITH THE WAIST. Without folding any edges over, sew a zigzag stitch around the waist, as close as possible to the fabric's raw edge. As you pass over the hip seams, fold both layers of the seam allowance to one side of the seam or the other. Make sure the crotch piece is pinned in its proper place, and sew around each leg hole with the zigzag stitch. As you get to the section where the crotch piece is pinned to the main piece, sew along the crotch piece as if it is just part of the front piece. Don't worry about the opening at the top of the crotch piece, as it will be sewn down on the sides.

Fold the edges under about 1/4" so that the raw edge is on the inside, and zigzag sew around all three openings again. Sew with the inside edge visible so that you can make this stitch "straddle" the raw edge. Make sure to fold over enough material to leave a tube casing for elastic to run through.

Repeat this step. Leave 3/4" unsewn, somewhere around the hips at each leg and leave 3/4" unsewn at the back of the waist. Now you have a slim tube of fabric around each hole, and you have an opening in each seam through which to feed the elastic.

Cut elastic cord into three pieces to go around the waist and each leg hole. Leave extra length on each. Attach a safety pin to one end of each elastic piece and feed it through each opening. Leaving the cord ends sticking out of the openings, and safety-pin the ends together to keep them from slipping back into the tube.

Now try on the undies, and cinch up the elastic wherever necessary, safety pinning the elastic to the right length. Cut off any extra elastic and then sew the elastic ends together. Try on again, then sew up those gaps in the seams where the cords went in.

With any luck, you've got yourself some fancy new one-of-a-kind underwear. If it's not what you expected, don't be discouraged! Try it again! My second attempts usually go much more according to plan, and sometimes the third try is the winner.

CRAFT MORE

✤ If you want to make some boxer-style underthings, you just need a different pattern. While they are somewhat easier because you only have to worry about elastic in the waist, the fly is tricky.

✤ I have used this method to make bathing suit bottoms. Any material that won't stretch (or shrink!) when it gets wet will work. A regular t-shirt will work if it's a dark color, and thick material. Test it under water first.

✤ If you want to make ruffles around the leg holes (which is very cute, but doesn't make for a subtle panty-line), you can sew the elastic directly to the inside of the undies, about 1/4" away from the edge. First fit the elastic around your leg to see how much you'll need. Do one round of hemming (fold edges under 1/4" and secure with zigzag stitch). Then pin the elastic to the inside of the leg hole by pinning first the end and the halfway point, then the 1/4 and 3/4 points, and so forth. This distributes the smaller circumference of elastic around larger circumference of the leg hole. Yes, this is tricky, but using lots of pins helps. As you sew, stretch the elastic to match the length of the leg hole edge; when you are done the elastic snaps back and you've got ruffles.

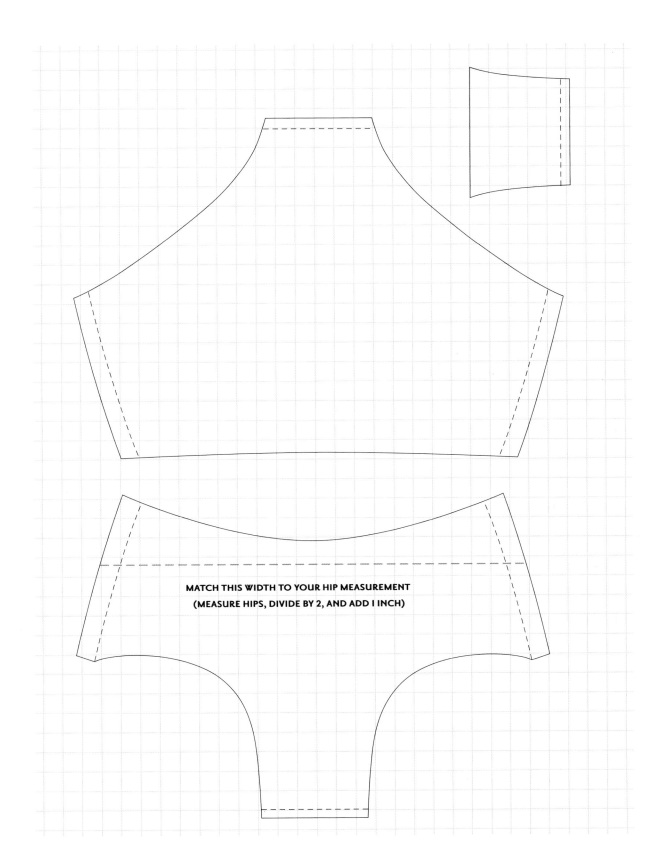

MATCH THIS WIDTH TO YOUR HIP MEASUREMENT
(MEASURE HIPS, DIVIDE BY 2, AND ADD I INCH)

Magic Lace Shawl

You'll Need:

Treasured textile fragments

Solvy™ stabilizer

A shawl, pashmina or shawl-size piece of wool jersey

Sewing thread in a color you would like to see running through your textile fragment and any other color for waste stitches you will rip

An iron

Wax paper

Sewing

Dressmaker's chalk pencil

Straight pins

BY SCOTT BODENNER

My mom has been collecting hand worked tatting, lace and linens for years. She once told me, "The women who made these had very sparse lives. This was what they did to make their world prettier and more personal." Hearing those words made me love these fabrics all the more.

I found the little bits of lacework on this shawl in an antique store and wanted to find a way to preserve their beauty but also make them usable for today. The magical Solvy™ was the answer. A plastic film that dissolves upon contact with water, Solvy™ is used as a stabilizer in sewing. You can stitch very delicate fabrics or create patterns on fabrics and then wash it away. When two layers are ironed together, they stick to each other, but not to paper or fabric. Solvy™ is tricky to sew over, being a sticky film, but you get a feel for it after a little while.

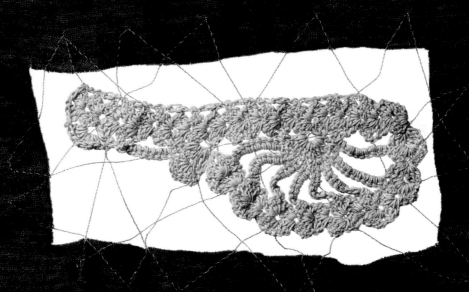

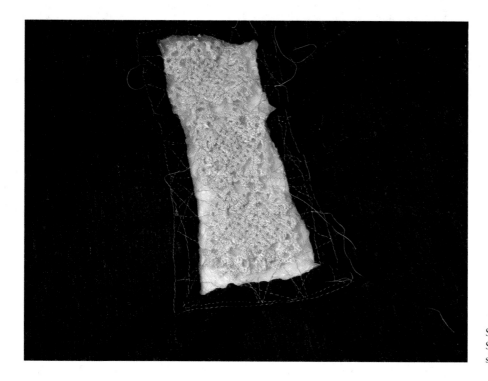

Shawl in progress with
Solvy™ and waste stitches
still in.

MAKING IT

1. Hand wash all your small lace fragments and the shawl and let them dry. You don't want any surprise running or shrinking. If you are working with wool jersey you can felt it so that you do not need to finish the edges. The shawl shown here was felted. (See page 82.)

2. Arrange your lace pieces on your shawl base in a pleasing pattern. Where you put your lace is where you will cut holes in your shawl.

3. With your dressmaker's pencil, mark where you will cut around your lace pieces giving them a 1"- to 2"- border.

4. Cut rectangular holes in shawl.

5. Cut 2 rectangles of Solvy™ 1" larger on all sides than the rectangular openings you've made.

6. Place a lace fragment between the layers of Solvy™.

7. Place Solvy™ with lace between two pieces of wax paper. Iron the Solvy™-wax paper "sandwich."

8. Remove the wax paper and use straight pins to pin the Solvy™ lace piece over hole in your shawl.

9. Now use sewing machine to stitch 1/2" around edge of hole in the waste thread color. This border stabilizes the Solvy™ and provides a boundary for the permanent stitches.

10. With the permanent color thread in the sewing machine, stitch back and forth over the lace using your waste stitch rectangle as the borders. You'll be creating a sort of web of stitching.

11. Hand wash gently and rip out the waste thread outline rectangle.

Tailor Made: Pearce Williams is small. At age sixteen, she began making her own clothes out of necessity and for pleasure. A decade later, her clothes now are perfectly tailored to her body and absolutely unique.

SHOWCASE

Silk Screen

BY JESSE ALEXANDER

Screen printing is just like stenciling except a screen is used to hold your stencil in place. If you are just getting started, it's much easier and reliable to buy pre-made frames from a craft, art supply or screen-printing store. Once you get a sense of how they work, it's easy to build your own out of wood or old window frames.

There are generally two types of screen-printing materials—monofilament and multifilament. Monofilament is finer and more uniform—great if you're working with a lot of detail. Multifilament is better if you are working with color blocks or thicker inks. Both come in a variety of gauges—the finer the gauge, the less ink that gets through. I've generally worked with 120-gauge monofilament fabric, but sometimes I've worked with other gauges (metallic ink, for example, needs something much less fine, like 60-gauge.)

SCREEN BLOCKS

You can use anything to block the screen from accepting ink (which is how you make a pattern): paper, glue, lacquer, tape, or a product called screen blocker that was created for this purpose. Duct tape is a great way to block a screen and create an interesting image—but make sure you adhere it to the underside of the screen, as adhering it to

the top side won't work. Remember also that duct tape doesn't last forever. If you need to wash out your screen to change inks, or if ink starts coming through in places you didn't want it to, stop, because the duct tape leakage will only get worse.

White letter, brown craft, notebook, or basic paper adhered to the screen with spray adhesive is a variation on tape that also works well, but again, make sure you adhere it to the underside of the screen.

White glue can be painted on to a screen to block oil-based inks and later taken off with water. Lacquer can be painted on to a screen to block water-based inks and later taken off with lacquer thinner.

INKS

If you are just starting out, there are plenty of off-the-shelf screen printing inks that will work great. If you want to branch out and make your own, keep in mind that it's easier to work with substances that

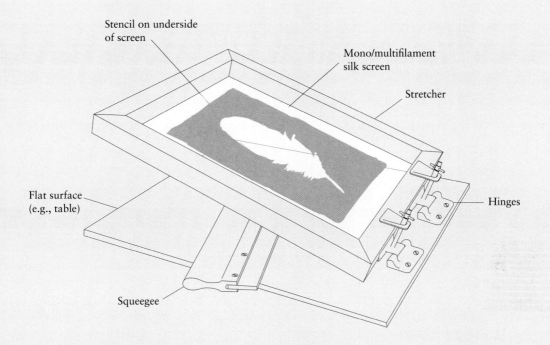

Stencil on underside
of screen

Mono/multifilament
silk screen

Stretcher

Flat surface
(e.g., table)

Hinges

Squeegee

have some thickness to them (so they don't spread or bleed unduly). Sodium alginate and several other substances known as thickening agents (available at craft stores) are wonderful goos that can be mixed with fabric dyes and then used as screen printing ink. It helps to read the dye manufacturer's instructions to see what they recommend you use in combination with their dyes to get the best saturation and longevity. I've had lots of luck with water-based inks that are a little less traditional. Anything you use that has the right consistency will work. I've used toothpaste, icing, even mud (which sometimes stains and sometimes doesn't), and all kinds of other gunk. You can get some really beautiful colors from some of the most unlikely things.

MORDANT

If you are using non-standard substances for print-making you usually need to use a mordant to make sure that the "dye" is held by the fabric. There are many kinds of mordant—ranging from alum to urine. (Yes, urine!) Some mordants are applied to the fabric, others are mixed with the dye, and sometimes you soak the printed fabric in the mordant after printing but before washing. Mordants can also affect the color of the dye—sometimes making it stronger or richer, and sometimes changing the color altogether. Many mordants are toxic, so read the labels for warnings. Wear rubber gloves. Extremely toxic dye mordants include sodium or ammonium dichromate, copper sulfate, ammonia and oxalic acid and I suggest you avoid them. Try using natural alternatives such as lemon juice, vinegar, bicarbonate of soda or sodium carbonate.

Poetic Silk Scarf

BY JESSE ALEXANDER

I first started screen printing fliers for my friends' bands when I was 19—I used some stuff my parents had in the basement, and soon expanded into t-shirts and posters. Later I started printing button-down shirts and duvets; it's easy to print on anything big and flat. But they were so heavy and expensive to ship, I wanted to find something that I could make and distribute cheaply. Silk scarves seemed like a natural. Scarves are iconic, and actually you can get the best resolution on satin.

You'll Need:

Apron and gloves

A big sink or a hose and a big basin

Silk or silk scarf

A standard 10" x 14" screen printing frame and squeegee

Duct tape, masking tape in several widths

Opaque fabric screen printing ink

Mordant (optional)

Several sizes of vinyl letters were silk screened on this scarf.

I tend to wear scarves as a cravat—I'm that kind of man. I saw this woman on the subway wearing one almost like a crown but she looked like an Egyptian sphinx and it made me think that that is really the only way to wear it. Actually scarves are so versatile, you can do whatever you want—halter tops, neck accouterments, diapers.

You can order blank, hand-rolled silk scarves at craft stores, or you can buy vintage silk scarves, which can be pretty cool and give you interesting ideas. You can also buy silk by the bolt at fabric or craft stores in a variety of colors and hand roll the scarves yourself—or don't roll them at all: it's not that important because they aren't washed that often and don't have stress point seams. Sometimes I just use yards of fabric as scarves—hemmed or just stitched around the edge. You could use other fabric, but silk (especially the satiny kind) works really well.

My process is totally experimental—sometimes I start with a concept (Led Zeppelin lyrics) or a process (marbleizing scarves with mustard). I have lots of ideas and most of them suck, so I try and weed through them before I get started.

MAKING IT

1. Build or buy a screen.

2. Create your pattern with masking tape or vinyl letters on the underside of the screen

3. Place the screen on the scarf. Tape or tack its underside to make sure that it is firmly in place.

4. Pour a generous amount of ink on top of the screen so that you can cover the screen in a fluid motion with the squeegee and use a squeegee, a spoon or your hand to force the ink through the screen onto the scarf.

5. Lift the screen. If you are doing multiple printings on a single scarf, reposition and repeat.

6. Set the scarf aside somewhere clean and out of the way. Let ink dry for however long instructions call for, soak in mordant, or rinse off (either according to the instructions for the ink you're using, or according to your instincts if you're in the experimental stage).

7. Wash your screen thoroughly

8. Rinse or wash repeatedly, until the ink is gone from the fabric.

9. Enjoy.

CRAFT MORE

✤ Many times I'm just too lazy to go through the whole silk screen process and I look for alternative methods to print on fabric. There are all sorts of wonderful objects to use to create simple block prints. I've used balled-up paper, my shoes, gnarly wood and lots of random things that were lying around at the time. The sneaker prints came out particularly well. I just looked at my feet and it made sense.

Classic Led Zeppelin lyrics make for a classic scarf.

A simple sneaker print evokes a Hermes scarf.

part 3

PAPER & PLASTIC

Gift Wraps

BY MALAINA NEUMANN

I have never enjoyed any craft that involves precision. Gift wrapping seems to be simple enough for monkeys to pull off, but I have wrapped some real stinkers in my time. They stuck out sorely under my mother's Christmas tree amongst the perfect bows and sparkly paper everyone else mustered up. And so... I vowed that even if I'm lazy, unprepared and not willing to spend the extra time that Martha Stewart would to create a beautifully wrapped gift, I can still give them something interesting to look at.

TORN PAPER WRAPPING

A design in torn paper won't take long to do and tearing things up seems strangely satisfying.

MAKING IT

1. Choose any shape to layer for an abstract look. Or try to tear out something specific: a bird or fish, hearts, arrows, etc. are easy.

2. For something fancy, say to wrap a mom-type of gift, do paper flowers. Tear petals from two light colored pieces of cardstock and piece them in a flower shape.

3. Tape flower shapes and leaves on base wrapping paper with scotch tape.

4. Any kind of paper looks extra pretty and soft with a sheet of tracing paper or vellum over it.

You'll Need:

Any kind of wrapping paper

Paper craft leaves

Scotch tape

Optional: tracing paper or vellum

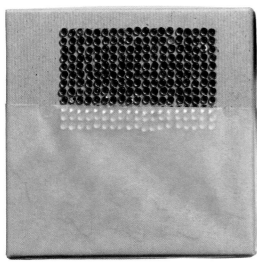

You'll Need:

A scarf that can fit nicely around your gift

Ribbon or even a hair elastic

Scissors

You'll Need:

One brown paper grocery bag

Assorted old magazines

Scotch tape or white glue

Scissors

SCARF WRAPPING

Use a scarf to create a one of a kind wrapping for a gift. It's like a little bonus gift!

MAKING IT

1. Lay out your scarf flat and put your gift in the center.

2. Gather the sides of the scarf together to the top middle of your box. Pull them tight and twist slightly.

3. Wrap your ribbon very tightly around the bottom of the twist and tie into a knot. Cut the ends short. Pull out and poof the scarf into a pleasing flower like shape.

RANSOM WRAPPING

Let's say you've put off wrapping or even getting the supplies until it's way, way too late. No sweat. A ransom note on paper bag is very punk rock, good for a boyfriend present.

MAKING IT

1. Cut a brown grocery bag to the size of your gift.

2. Wrap.

3. Cut an assortment of letters from magazines. Arrange them to spell out the recipient's name, and, of course, your name. Easy as pie!

CRAFT MORE

✤ Coat your lips with your best lipstick shade and kiss a sheet of tissue paper silly.

✤ Use tin foil. We've all done it. Or the comics. Or the racy section of the personal ads taking time to circle your favorites. There is nothing wrong with recycling last year's wrapping paper, artsy newspaper pages, or maps.

✤ Cover any plainly wrapped gift with something, anything, and make it special. The scrap booking aisles at the craft stores are loaded with ideas, but star stickers, googly eyes, and flat, vintage buttons work nicely.

✤ Apply any paper craft (stamping, embossing, origami, torn paper, collage, decoupage) to your package for instant beauty.

✤ A special gift tag can really perk up a package. I found some sweet pictures in an old children's book that I cut out, wrote the name of the recipient on and taped to the gift.

✤ Don't forget the ribbons! Retro cloth ribbon looks great, so does raffia.

Ocean Marbleized Paper: Jesse Alexander just may be the Johnny Knoxville of craft. After trying puddles, parking lots, and pools, he finally marbleized a 12' x 100' roll of black paper in the ocean (using biodegradable inks, of course) with a little help from some friends.

S·H·O·W·C·A·S·E

Shrink Plastic Necklace

You'll Need:

A package of clear shrink plastic (there are several different brands available)

A regular hole punch

Scissors

An oven or toaster oven

Paintbrush, acrylic varnish and acrylic paints in your choice of colors (the necklace shown was made from one base color of violet and then mixed with white, grey and black paints to create varying hues)

Necklace cord. The one shown is suede, but you can use anything you please, from ribbon to hemp to leather. You'll need about 2' depending on where you want the necklace to hang—experiment to find the right length. Suede or ribbon will be easy to tie into a knot or bow around your neck. If you choose leather or hemp, you may also want to get some crimps with necklace clasps, which can be found at any bead or craft store.

BY JESSICA POUNDSTONE

It's unlikely that you've done much thinking about Shrinky Dinks since you were a kid. Well neither had I—until about a year ago.

It all started when I saw an artistic pendant made from Fimo clay. "Cool! I want to do that!" I thought. So off I went to the craft store for the first time in ages. I found the clay, and started to read the instructions on the package. With each line I became more disheartened. I'd had no idea the clay would be so high maintenance. As soon as I got to the part about how "you may want to use a pasta machine to ensure clay is of uniform thickness and bakes evenly" I bailed. I do not now own, nor do I ever plan to own, a pasta machine. And I didn't want to use a medium that seemed so cranky and demanding.

So, roaming around the store to see what else was new in the land of craft, I ran across a product called Shrinky Dinks. Could these be the same Shrinky Dinks from my youth? Indeed, they were! Why not make a pendant out of this stuff? I wondered. I decided to give the "Frosted Ruff N' Ready" sheets a try.

That night, and many nights to follow, my house became a jewelry-making factory. I couldn't get enough. Although the house was becoming overpopulated with colorful earrings and pendants, I was still hesitant to wear any of the jewelry out. What if people asked what it was made from? "Shrinky Dinks" hardly sounds elegant. Eventually I got over it, and started wearing the jewelry everywhere, partly as a way to inject some color into my primarily brown and black wardrobe. Everywhere I wore it, people asked about it, and even offered to buy it. So I started selling it. Now here I am living happily ever after, having decked myself and people across the world in Shrinky Dink jewelry.

You're next.

MAKING IT

1. Use the templates on the opposite page to cut four concentric circles from your sheets of shrink plastic.

2. Punch a hole in the largest circle with your hole punch. Make sure it's centered, and that the top of the hole is about 1/4" away from the top of the plastic. Use this hole as a guide to punch holes in the other circles so that they all line up.

3. Bake your circles, following the package instructions. If necessary, flatten the circles under a heavy book or board while they're still warm.

4. Paint the rough side of each circle. If you're using a lighter color, you may want to do two coats. Once dry, add a coat of acrylic varnish to seal in the color. Let the varnish dry.

5. Set your circles on top of each other and thread cord through all of the holes. Lining up the ends of your cord with your circles at the fold, tie an overhand knot about 1" from the circles. It's important to leave some extra cord in a loop between the plastic circles and the knot so you're not fanning the circles out by pulling the knot tight right up against the plastic. To hold the cord around your neck, tie the ends in a bow or knot—or use crimps and clasps for a more "finished" look.

6. Tie on your big, bold, easy-to-assemble necklace and wait for the compliments to roll in!

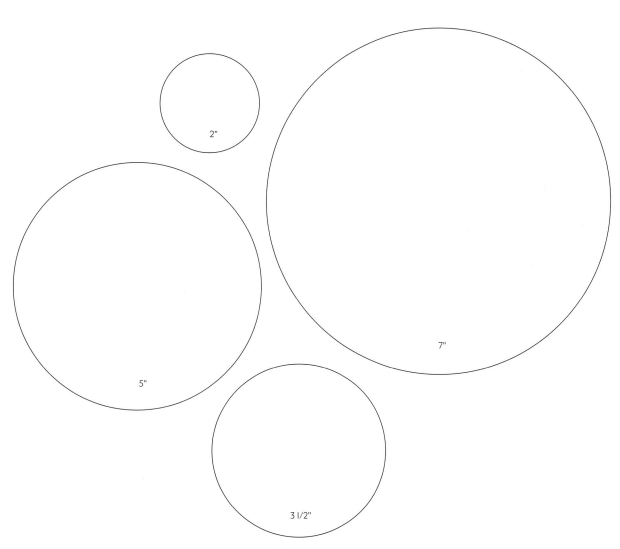

2"

7"

5"

3 1/2"

Pattern actual size.

Cut Paper Mobile

BY JESSE ALEXANDER

I made this mobile for a friend's baby, because I wanted her to grow up with an appreciation of New York's detritus. It's easy to be scared of the city's flotsam and jetsam, but it's beautiful if you are open to it. It took me a day, using mostly stuff that I had on hand. They say babies like contrast, so a black mobile is actually ideal. They will see it against a lighter colored ceiling in their room. Making a mobile is an entirely open ended process. It's about playing with balance—you can add things endlessly, but everything you add immediately affects the whole, so you have to move between spontaneity and forethought. The first mobile I made was very complicated—lots and lots of branches and movement. After that I simplified things a little—sometimes it's nice to be simple-minded. Indoor mobiles should be light, so they can catch even minor breezes and movement of the air. Outdoor mobiles need to be more rugged.

You'll Need:

Scissors

Cardboard or heavy construction paper that won't curl

Thread, thin wire or string

Needle

Wire snips

Coat hanger or wire of about the same gauge, a few feet at most

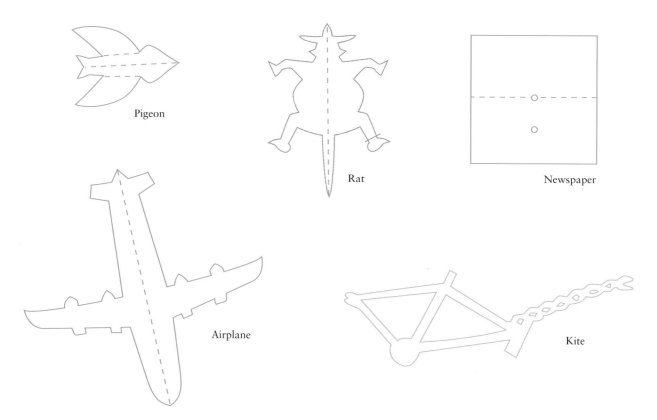

Pigeon

Rat

Newspaper

Airplane

Kite

MAKING IT

1. Draw and cut out some simple shapes out of paper. You can use the patterns on these pages or create your own. I used 65-l black construction paper. You can also make some lightweight three-dimensional paper objects such as paper airplanes or cranes. Start by making about eight to ten shapes.

2. Attach a thin piece of string or thread or wire to each one. You can do this by wrapping thread around the thinnest part of the object so it hangs or punching a hole in the paper or cardboard with a pin. Leave the thread long (you can always cut it later).

3. Set up something to hang your mobile on as you're building it. If you are making a mobile for a particular location you could work right there, but you can also just hang it temporarily from a yardstick taped to the top of a bookshelf.

4. Make the basic structure for the mobile. A coat hanger works pretty well—you get a build-in hook. If you cut the coat hanger with the wire snips in the middle of the bottom then you have a very nice initial structure to start with.

5. Use string and wire to make a few more branches on the base.

6. Begin to tie the paper ornaments to the structure of the mobile. It's a very organic process—as you add objects you may find that you need to add or subtract branches, and you may find that you have too many or not enough ornaments.

Continue to add ornaments. Play with the balance. Jiggle and blow on it to see how it moves.

CRAFT MORE

✢ Random light objects make good mobile material—try cocktail umbrellas, matchbooks, cut up postcards, and snapshots for the older set.

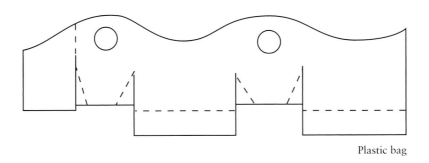

Plastic bag

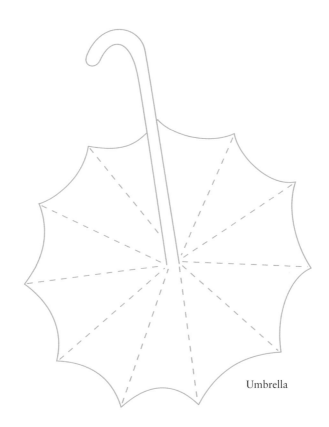

Umbrella

Patterns actual size.

Graffiti Rubber Doormat

BY RODGER STEVENS

Somewhere in the vicinity of ten years old, I started noticing the names and phrases written on the surfaces of walls, trains, and billboards. The hundreds of little black marker tags seemed sinister, but the big, bold, bulging graffiti letters were just spectacular. My opinion on matters of graffiti has since grown more complicated and nuanced, but my initial impressions are more or less intact. It still strikes me as a shame that all that hard work rarely gets to bask in the public eye before being buffed, scraped, painted over, or otherwise attacked. In an effort to combat the forces of eradication and to pay tribute to the gorgeousness of those criminal letters, I set about to make a work of graffiti that could be rolled up and taken home, where it could spend its life happy and appreciated. Of course, I didn't want to wrench the art form from its natural habitat completely, so I made it floor-bound, where it can still get trampled by the general public.

You'll Need:

A smooth or striated rubber mat of roughly 1/8" thickness. The length and width will depend on you; I started with a sheet approximately 30" x 70". Rolls of this stuff are available at most large home-repair stores and stores specializing in industrial floor-coverings.

Chalk or colored pencils in a color contrasting that of the rubber.

A heavy-duty utility knife. These knives are designed to cut difficult materials like linoleum and vinyl. They are mostly handled, with a small triangular blade, and are available in any hardware or art supply store.

There are countless reasons why you should endeavor to make one of these things: the unparalleled education in letter forms that the study of graffiti provides; the sheer joy of pulling a sharp blade through freshly milled rubber; and the importance of working on your hands and knees once in a while, to name a few. But the best reason is simply because it is always more rewarding to make something than not to.

1. First, spend some time being alert to bits of graffiti everywhere you go. Take pictures of the most interesting ones.

2. With your inspiration spread out before you, roll out a sheet of commercial-grade rubber matting. Work on the floor or any other surface large enough and steady enough to accommodate the entire piece. Your utility blade should be sharp, which means that whatever is under the mat will also be cut up, so either protect that surface or be willing to live with its new texture.

3. With a waxy colored pencil (Prismacolors are nice) or a piece of sidewalk chalk, trace out a conglomeration of plump letters, making sure that they are all kissing or overlapping sufficiently.

4. Using a heavy-duty utility knife, cut out the pattern you've drawn. Cutting a sheet of rubber is not unlike cutting matte board or very heavy paper: there is some resistance, but once the blade is in, it will move through the material without much difficulty. To make the cut, put the knife's point into the rubber at a 45-degree angle; press down firmly until the blade is fully through. Then pull the blade along your traced line with enough pressure to cut, not simply score, the rubber mat.

Step back, take a moment to admire your work, walk across the thing, and go eat a piece of fruit.

Pattern approximately
1/5 actual size.

Button Cuff

You'll Need:

45 1/4" four-holed shirt buttons, for an average-sized cuff of 15 buttons and three rows (number of buttons depends on desired width of cuff, though 15 buttons for each row is my standard for length)

Spool of heavy cotton thread—tatting or crochet cotton thread works well, though your color choices are limited; heavy quilting or button thread also works fine

Darning needle

Satin ribbon thin enough to lace through a tiny button hole

BY ANNETTE KESTERSON

For as long as I can remember, the women in my family have had big coffee cans full of buttons sort of loitering around, waiting for something to happen. The tendency has diffused through the generations, and neither my mother nor I feel compelled to cut all the shirt buttons off something before it gets thrown in the rag-bag. But the fascination with the beautiful and useful button lingers on in my completely un-domestically-inclined heart. When I started trying to figure out what I wanted to do with my button stash, I was a renegade without a plan, but I have since seen some lovely pieces made of buttons, including amazing tote bags that are well beyond my attention span and patience. I have made several baskets, large and small, with the same technique, but the cuffs are my favorite button pieces thus far; I love that they are simple and wholesome but also elegant.

1. Lay out buttons in three rows of 15. You will see that each button has two vertical holes and two horizontal holes. Orient buttons so that the holes make a diamond shape instead of a square.

2. Begin your first row of buttons. Anchor the thread to the first button by knotting thread in loop around "outside" buttonhole —that is the left horizontal hole. This will end up being one open side of your cuff. I used doubled thread, and added lengths with a half-hitch through the old loop for a continuous length with the smallest visible join.

3. Push thread through the right horizontal hole to the anchor and then down through the left horizontal hole of the next button, then back up through the same right horizontal hole in the first button. Loop through those two linking holes twice, ending on the back side of the two buttons, making sure the buttons are drawn up tightly together and that they lie flat.

4. "Girdle" the loop that connects the two buttons by tightly winding the thread twice around the connecting loop, then coming back up through the right horizontal buttonhole of the second button.

5. Connect that button to the third button in the same manner as you connected the first to the second, continuing until the final button in the row. Two loops should connect each button, with two loops around the connections to strengthen the bond and make it look neater.

6. When you have finished the first row of buttons, things may seem trickier. Don't worry—it's the same process, and you're pretty much a pro once you've made your first row. Now double check your row. All the buttons in the first row should be oriented so the holes in the button are in a diamond shape, not a square, and there is thread connecting each button through the two horizontal holes in the diamond. Repeat 2 more times.

7. Now you will join 2 chains by creating the horizontal joins. Turn your 2 chains 180-degrees so they are now vertical. All the vertical holes should be connected.

8. Begin by threading your new thread through the back of the top loop that secures your right vertical chain. Bring your thread from back to front through the left horizontal hole of your right chain.

9. Thread front to back through the right horizontal hole of your left chain, now connecting the two chains. Repeat 2 more times and then girdle twice ending at the back of the work.

10. Pull the thread through the right chain bottom vertical connection under the girdle, so it blends in and appears neat.

11. Thread through back to front to the right chain left horizontal hole. Now you are in position to loop and girdle as you did in step 9. Repeat for the number of buttons.

12. At the end of the chain, thread your horizontal join thread through the right bottom vertical sewing loop on the back of the work.

13. Tie off the last button securely, and shape the cuff to your wrist. Lace ribbon in a criss-cross pattern connecting two edges and tie in a bow to secure on your wrist. To put on and take off the cuff, just loosen the laces—no need to re-lace every time.

CRAFT MORE

✤ I prefer buttons to be exactly the same size for this project, but if you are more casual in your attitude toward symmetry, you can use different buttons in the project, as long as you relax the tension. I like my stuff to be rigid and clean, but by building in some slack a "floppy" version can be made with a variety of different buttons. Or you can use the same size and style of buttons in different colors for variety.

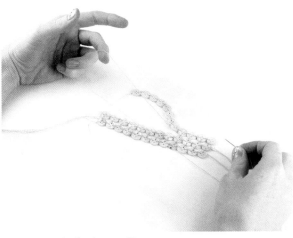

Connecting the final row of buttons.

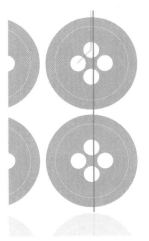

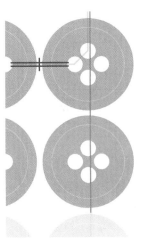

Thread new thread through back of top loop.

Girdle the two chains together.

✤ You can join the sides of your cuff using elastic thread rather than the ribbon and bow for ease of wearing—it does get tricky tying that bow all on your own sometimes!

✤ Instead of thread, you can use 28-gauge wire in copper, silver, or finish of your choice—I work in lengths of about a yard, trying to leave 6" long tails at the ends of rows rather than joining in the middle of a chain. Gather all loose tails at the rows and coil together. These will become a hook and eye closure. I joined my wire cuffs with a sort of "shabby chic" approach to the hook and loop closure. To make a hook, cut a piece of new wire about 1 1/2" long. Combine ends and new wire, about 3" long, to make a twist of 4-6 strands of wire trimmed to an even length, bended to make a hook at one end. On the other side, bend your ends into a loop. Insert hook into loop et voilá. Or you could bind the wire and attach a regular jewelry closure to your project using jump rings or the wire itself to attach.

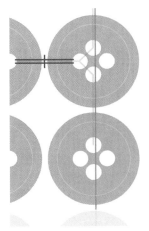

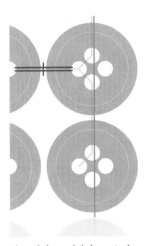

Pull the thread through the right chain bottom vertical hole.

Thread through left vertical hole, and you are ready to girdle the next button.

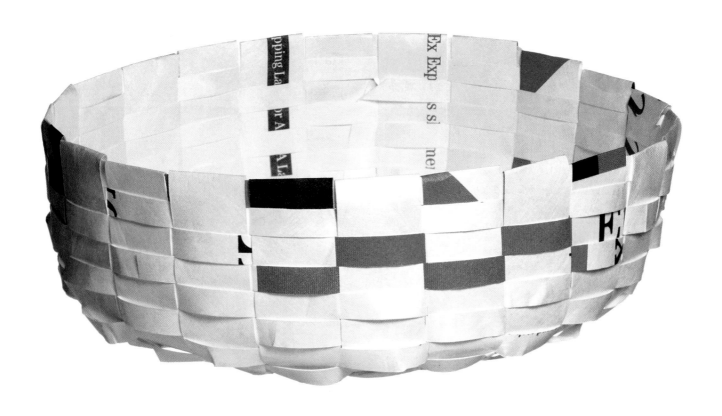

Tyvek Basket

BY DAVID RAINBIRD

Indestructible, waterproof, and lightweight, Tyvek is the wonder material you get free in the mail—the United States Postal Service, UPS, and Fedex all use Tyvek envelopes for overnight delivery. Tyvek was originally developed by accident in 1955 when a DuPont engineer spied some of the material's trademark white fluff spilling out of a tube in the lab. After nearly a decade of research, the company named it Tyvek, and now it's actually going through a bit of a renaissance. Used for far more than just rip-proof envelopes and house siding, Tyvek has become a cool material thanks, in part, to the efforts of Nike (they've made a running shoe from it that's designed to last for one marathon), Tord Boontje (stylish lace curtains with cutouts of deer and bunnies)—and now, craftivists everywhere. Here's how to make your own white Tyvek basket with either orange and purple, brown or blue and red accents, depending on your corporate supplier.

You'll Need:

| I 12" x 15" Tyvek mailing envelope |
| Scissors |
| Thick 15" square cardboard |
| Map pins |
| Paper clips |

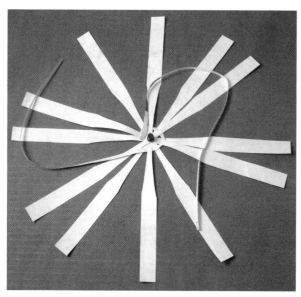

Weave a thin weaver in a tight circle around five stakes close to the center.

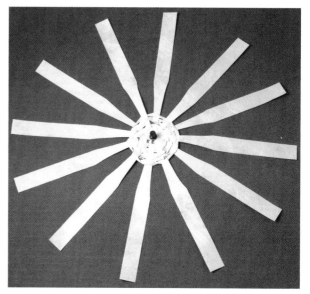

Tuck each end of the weaver in parallel to one of the stakes.

MAKING IT

1. Cut the Tyvek envelope into the following pieces:
   + 12 stakes: 14" x 3/4"
   + 8 thin weavers: 30" x 3/16"
   + 6 thick weavers: 30" x 1/4"

2. Fold stakes in half to mark the middle. With scissors, cut each stake so it tapers 3" from the fold until they are 1/4" thick in the middle.

3. Arrange six stakes in a clock face pattern on a piece of thick cardboard and hold them in place in the middle with a map pin.

4. Fold a thin weaver in half around one of the stakes near the pin. Take the half that lies under the stake and weave it in a tight circle around the other five stakes. Because the weaver is straight, you will need to fold the weaver again and again as you follow the stakes around the circle.

5. When you have completed one round, take the other half of the weaver and weave it over and under the opposite stakes. Then tuck each end of the weaver into the weaving, parallel with one of the stakes.

6. Arrange the remaining six stakes between the existing ones and use the map pin to hold all 12 in place.

7. Fold a second thin weaver around the stake at the same place where the first weaver left off. Continue weaving.

8. When you've finished with a weaver, tuck it into the weaving parallel with one of the stakes and tuck the beginning of another weaver into the weaving on the next stake.

9. Continue weaving this way with thin weavers until you have made a circle about 5 1/2" in diameter. Cut the ends of the thin weavers and tuck them into the weaving.

10. Now start weaving with two thick weavers. Don't fold these weavers. Instead allow them to pull the stakes up toward a vertical position. Use paper clips every few stakes to hold the weavers in place. After about three rows of the thick weaver, you'll be weaving the sides of the basket.

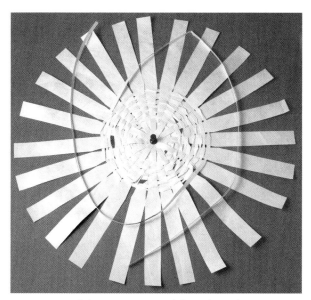

Weave a second thin weaver around the stake and continue weaving.

Weave with the thick weavers to make the sides of the basket.

Fold the stakes down to tuck them in, alternating inside and outside the basket.

11. After about eight rows (or whatever height you'd like your basket), finish each weaver on the same stake, tucking one into the weaving on the inside and one into the weaving on the outside of the basket. Tapering the thick weavers over the last few inches will make the basket more even. To do this, cut the weaver with scissors so that the last few inches get gradually thinner, almost to a point. If you don't taper them, the top edge of the basket will be a bit uneven.

12. Finally, fold the stakes down over the top row of weavers (alternately inside and outside the basket) and tuck them into the weaving. This finishes and strengthens the basket. Put the basket out for the postman to put your mail in—though that might be a bit flagrant in flaunting your basket's origins. It also works well for apples.

part 4

GLASS
CERAMIC

You'll Need:

A rectangular picture frame with glass large enough for a playing board (I used an 18" x 24" frame)

Acrylic paint. You will need 2 contrasting colors to create the different sides of the board. If you don't already have acrylic paint, two very small tubes will suffice. (I used Liquitex High Viscosity acrylic paints in Phthalocyanine Blue and Cerulean Blue and mixed a little iridescent silver into them for luster.)

Small paint brushes

Illustration board larger than the picture frame by 1"

Wrapping paper or any pretty paper larger than your frame by at least 1". (I used printed Japanese rice paper.)

Spray fixative

2 colors Krylon glossy spray enamel (I used navy and light blue.)

Balsa wood, at least as long as the shortest inside dimension of your frame and 3/4" wide and 3/16" thick

Elmer's or other wood-to-glass glue

An existing backgammon board or use stencil on page 135

Newspapers

Backgammon pieces or anything circular that is the right size (coins, poker chips, cut plastic)

Dice

Backpainted Glass Backgammon Board

BY DOUGLAS RICCARDI

My backgammon obsession has had its ups and downs since its start in the tenth grade. When my friend Emily brought her board to my beach shack one summer, the obsession was rekindled with a vengeance. I also started searching for the perfect board. The stores carried the usual suspects, inlaid woods, marbleized plastic, various colors of leather—nothing was right. I had in mind something with the panache of one I had seen in Milan—a beautiful oversized affair in clear, red and black lucite. It was 500 Euros, and that was way too much.

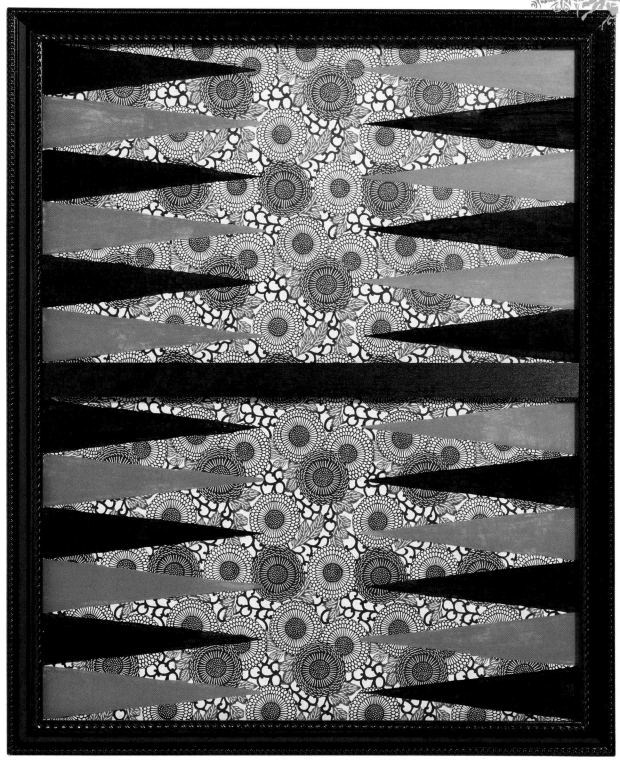

Luckily that summer also brought out the craftier side in me and my cottage guests and the thought crossed our minds to make our own. The first attempt was made of found beach wood, milk paint, and branches cut in slices for the pieces. A little too rustic.

I had always wanted to try a back-painted glass project because it is really very magical. This was the perfect opportunity. Finding the perfect frame was the biggest challenge until a photograph frame solved all my problems—the glass was pre-cut, and the sides were high enough that the dice were contained on the surface.

MAKING IT

1. Remove the glass from the frame.

2. Lay the frame on top of newspaper in a well-ventilated area. Spray paint it with the navy gloss enamel. Do several light coats and allow sufficient time to dry between coats.

3. Spray paint balsa with same enamel.

4. Use pattern on the opposite page or an existing board. Lay it underneath the glass. Paint on your triangles or points in alternating colors of the acrylic paint. Again, do a few light coats, allowing them to dry between coats. At first, the paint may appear too thin but once it is on an opaque surface, you will see the desired effect.

5. Spray the same side of the glass that you painted on with spray adhesive.

6. Spray the wrong side of the wrapping paper with spray adhesive. Adhere the wrapping paper to the illustration board by laying it in the middle of the board and smoothing it out toward the sides. Using the piece of glass as a guide, trim excess paper to size. You put this piece behind the glass in the frame as the backing.

7. Reassemble your frame, wrapped illustration board, and glass with the painted side down.

8. Glue in balsa wood divider on the top side in the middle of the board.

9. Spray paint backgammon pieces in two colors, 15 of each color.

10. Get out your dice and play backgammon.

CRAFT MORE

✤ Make a checkers or chess board using the same technique.

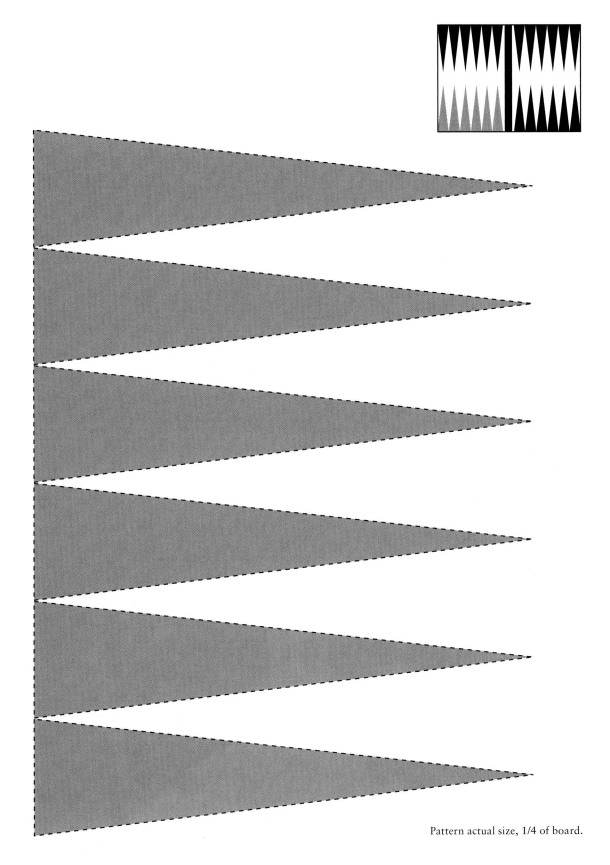

Pattern actual size, 1/4 of board.

Glass Dining Table

BY JENNIFER KABAT AND DAVID RAINBIRD

Living in the country there isn't a whole lot to do on a Saturday night. The nearest movie theater is an hour away so instead we head to our local auction house. Before you laugh, you should know a few things about Roberts' Auction. 1. It serves the best apple pie you've ever had. 2. It's like Christie's meets *Deliverance* (an odd combo of high, low and hick in the sticks), where the entertainment fun is all headed up by one Eddie Roberts, a salty guy who looks like he came out of an Annie Proulx novel. He's agelessly worn like a pair of old jeans, which indeed he does always wear along with a belt sporting a buckle the size of a splayed hand and a just-too-tight shirt. The man is a style icon. 3. The fun starts at 7 pm sharp, so you need to come early to check out all the goods.

You'll Need:

A second hand wood dining table with expandable leaves

A hammer and patience

Heavy duty screws or epoxy glue

Electric drill

4 heavy duty rubber non-slip furniture pads

A glass table top, I/2" to 3/4" thick, with finished edges and rounded corners, the size of the existing wood table top with all the leaves in place

Roberts' Auction house, like all such places purveying the dust and detritus of other people's lives, is a deeply inspirational place. You can find Victorian photo albums and 1960's pop-art posters from London (how they got to the Catskills is beyond us). You look at the goods not for what they are—a broken down old table for instance—but rather for how you can transform it. Thus we came up with our glass-topped table. We were inspired by the elaborately tooled legs but found the glossy, polished wooden table top a bit too grandma. So we decided to ditch the shiny top, keep the legs, and top it all with a big old slab of glass instead.

This is a fairly easy craft project but there are some things to bear in mind. The legs will be bearing a lot of weight. A suitable piece of glass for the top will be 1/2" to 3/4" thick and obviously the size of a dining room table so that makes it very heavy.

So check out the table to see how stable it is. You don't just want four legs that screw into the table top. You need the legs themselves to have a supporting structure independent of the top, so that if they don't have a table top on them they still stand up. Thus the legs form a sturdy base for the glass top that rests on them.

Ours was an expanding table, so we permanently extended the expansion mechanism to support the glass. And depending on your mechanism, this bit can be a feature too, a bit like seeing inside the old steam engine in a science museum. The mechanism has cool sliding cogs and widgets, so we flipped it over so you could see all the weird whirligigs through the glass top.

We ordered our glass online. You want the edges finished so they're not sharp, and also slightly rounded corners. If you order online you can find off-the-shelf glass table tops in many designs but if you have fancy legs, a simpler top looks pretty stylish. As far as size goes, follow the original table size or just slightly larger. If you make it too big, it risks being top-heavy.

MAKING IT

1. Remove the wooden top from your table. This may mean pulling out nails or screws depending on how the table was put together. You only need the bottom part of the table. Be gentle. You may want to reinforce with L-brackets using an electric drill when you are done.

2. Extend the table, without its top, to its maximum size. Remove the expansion mechanisms. These will provide arms to help support the glass. You may need to clean them up. After a century's worth of grime and dinners being eaten over them, they can be dusty and full of crumbs.

3. Use screws or very strong glue to fix the expansion arms in place so they can't close. Use your drill and heavy-duty screws to attach the arms to the leg/base structure.

4. Place the four rubber pads on the arms to make sure your glass stays in place.

5. Place glass top on top of the table. It weighs a ton and so will stay in place without any fastening system.

6. Eat dinner.

SHOWCASE

Broken Glass Chandelier: British glass artist Deborah Thomas makes chandeliers out of broken glass she finds at flea markets and thrift stores. Deftly wired together, they are magnificent.

Etched Pitcher and Glasses

I think this project came from a sublimated urge to get a tattoo, which I don't have although I've thought about it for years. Etching a pattern is a great way to wrap some glassware in mystery. And unlike inking a rose on your ankle, it makes a thoughtful housewarming gift.

You'll Need:

4-8 glasses and a pitcher

Utility knife (Exacto) and extra blades (you want to work with a very sharp blade)

Printable adhesive paper or plastic (8 1/2" x 11" for printers)

Masking tape

Scissors

Glass etching cream

A cream applicator (in layman's terms: a cheap small brush)

Chemical resistant gloves and goggles

Glass cleaner

Paper towels

A couple of used jars or bottles for practice

Glass

MAKING IT

1. Get your desired patterns onto adhesive paper or plastic. You can photocopy the pattern on these pages or you can download and print them from our site. Make several copies so you can practice.

2. Clean your glass surface really well. Really, really well. Clean it again.

3. Adhere your pattern to your glass or pitcher. The paper acts as a mask to prevent the etching cream from etching where you don't want it. Use a nice big piece so that you have a big work area. It cannot have bubbles or wrinkles; otherwise the etching cream will seep through the stencil and it will look sloppy. This is why the practice jars are so important.

4. Cut out your stencil. This is the most tedious part of the project. You want your blade always to be very sharp (watch your fingers) so you will probably want to replace your blade a couple of times as you cut out your stencils. As soon as your blade snags on the adhesive paper it is time to switch. You may want to peel up parts of your stencil as you go. You can carefully begin the peeling process with the tip of the knife. If, at the end, you think that you don't have enough of the glass covered, then extend the mask with masking tape. Smooth down the edges of the stencil to really secure it to the glass.

5. Wipe away all fingerprints on the areas that will be etched. Rubbing alcohol works well. Fingerprints can ruin the etch.

6. Take all your materials to a well-ventilated area. Put down newspaper on your work surface. Make sure you are wearing protective, long-sleeved clothes.

7. Read the instructions for the etching cream. Most creams require a shake or a stir and 15 minutes to work.

8. Put on your gloves. Follow the directions for your etching cream. Apply a thin layer of the etching cream to the open area of the stencil with a brush. Do not slop it on. This stuff eats through things, so if you put a bunch on the edge of your adhesive paper, chances are, you will get a fuzzy edge. Definitely use a practice jar the first time around.

9. After the specified time, rinse off your glass and peel away the paper. You should have a beautiful etched glass in your hand. Salut!

Pitcher spout

Pitcher body

Enlarge stencils as needed.

The Chandy

BY SCOTT BODENNER

I rather like a bare bulb in a plain ceramic socket, but then it also seems a little naked. My sister has a physical aversion to the bare bulb, and I never want her to feel uncomfortable in my house. This project was the solution to the bare bulb in my bathroom.

I drew this design from beaded Victorian bulb jackets, made when electric lights were first entering the market. Light fixtures still used bulbs like candles and just left them exposed. The body of Victorian chandeliers was ornate metal, which I think made for a very confusing contrast. I love the bead jacket solution—so pretty, yet gawky, in a charming way.

You'll Need:

9 large drop crystals (vintage or new). These can vary in shape. Mine were no longer than 1 1/2".

About 40 small crystals, mixed width of 1/2" and 3/4", each with two holes in them

1/4" jump rings, 4-5 dozen

Needle-nose pliers

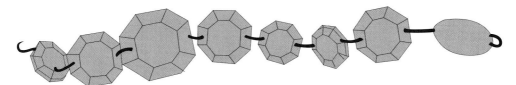

Make a necklace of crystals long enough to go around the neck of the lightbulb but small enough to not fall off when on the bulb with larger glass bits hanging off.

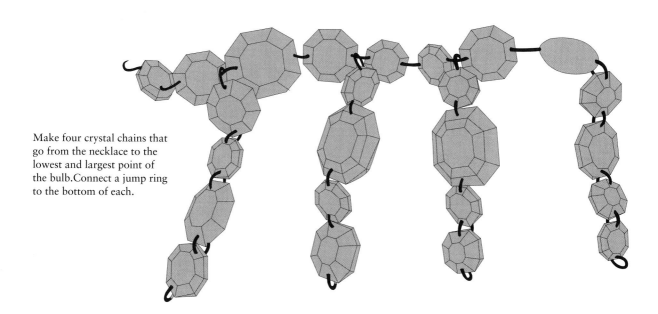

Make four crystal chains that go from the necklace to the lowest and largest point of the bulb. Connect a jump ring to the bottom of each.

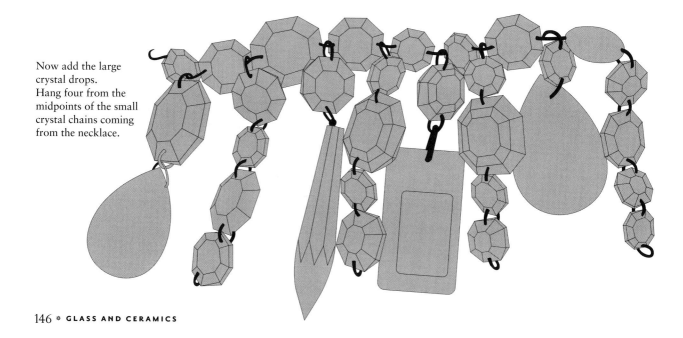

Now add the large crystal drops. Hang four from the midpoints of the small crystal chains coming from the necklace.

Connect all your long crystal strands together and finish with a medium crystal and a large drop.

MAKING IT

1. Vintage crystals often have metal bits still attached, so the first step is to remove these metal bits using needle-nose pliers.

2. Next, attach a jump ring to each crystal, large and small. Jump rings make a uniform and tidy connecting system. Be careful not to open jump rings like Pac Man opens his mouth, from an O to a C. This makes it very hard to close the ring again. A better method is to use the pliers to gently twist them open along the other axis, tourqueing the two ends.

3. Make a necklace of crystals long enough to go around the neck of the light bulb but small enough to not fall off when the bulb has the larger glass drops hanging off.

4. Make four evenly spaced crystal chains that hang down from the necklace to the lowest and largest point of the bulb. On a regular bulb these chains will be four to five crystals each. Connect a jump ring to the bottom of each.

5. Now add the large crystal drops. Hang four in between your crystal chains.

6. Connect your four chains together and finish with a medium crystal and a large drop.

7. For ease of removal when you have to change the bulb, use a wire to make a hook on one end of the necklace that can go through a closed jump ring. I have made a pattern that fits a standard light bulb. You can adjust the length and circumference with additional small crystals for a specialty bulb. Note that four chains of crystals each end with a jump ring. These are connected by a single jump ring so they encircle the bottom of the bulb.

8. Take a bath and marvel at the beauty you just added to your life hanging from the ceiling of your bathroom.

Glass Mosaic Trivets

You'll Need:

8" square piece of wood, plywood, or MDF board

Round headed glass or tile nippers

3 sheets, each 8 1/2" x 11", of stained glass in at least 3 colors (available in craft shops)

Premixed sanded grout in grey OR house paint tints in black and dark blue

Clear glass glue (check which glass glue works with your surface material)

Newspaper

Gardening gloves

Goggles

Paper bowls

1" to 3" spackling knife

Small house paintbrush

Grout spreader

Grouting sponge

BY LESLIE LINKSMAN

For a while I made wind chimes. They made beautiful sounds but I wanted to bring light into the equation. So I began to make wind chimes that used glass beads and had mosaic tops. This is how I started doing mosaics. They were quite time consuming to make and let's just say there isn't a lot of money to be made in the wind chime business. However, many times people would ask me if I could mosaic something else for them— an end table, a coffee table and once a claw foot bathtub. I was happy to agree.

1. Set up your workspace to avoid getting small bits of glass all over your house. Lay down your newspaper with a stack of bowls, your nippers, and your glass sheets handy.

2. Don your gloves and goggles.

3. Cut the glass with your nippers. You move the nippers over where you want the cut to occur and squeeze. The best technique is to take your sheet of glass and cut it in the center. Set one half aside. Cut the other half in the center again. Set one of the halves aside. Now you should have a piece of glass easier to handle. Over your bowl nip the glass into roughly 1" by 2" rectangles. They will be irregular in shape and that is fantastic. You can eyeball as you go along if you think you have enough to cover your surface. You want to cut your 3 colors so you can make a unique pattern. Keep each color in separate bowls.

4. Wrap the extra glass in newspaper and put away. Carefully roll up your newspaper to avoid spreading glass shards and discard. Vacuum up if you are in an indoor space. Lay down a new set of newspaper.

5. Now arrange your tiles on your surface to see what you think is pretty. You may need to keep gloves on through this process. The glass is sharp, so be careful. You do not want more than a 1/4" of grout between your pieces. It is more pleasing to have your tiles closer together. Ideally, your joints should be 1/8". This makes wiping off the grout easier.

6. Remove your glass and brush on your glue. Follow the directions. It usually takes a long time to dry so you can apply glue and still move your tiles around. For larger projects you may want to glue down in sections. Press the glass pieces into the glue so it adheres well. Do not use so much glue that it oozes around the sides when you press down. Use only enough to cover the tile so you feel it adhere and sink slightly onto the substrate. Try to keep the tiles as level and as flat as possible.

7. Allow it to dry for as long as your glue directions state. Test it by touching a tile. If it moves even a little, it is not dry. If it pops off, re-glue using more glue.

8. Spread your grout (or grout you've mixed with house paint tint) over the glass tiles. Use your spackling knife to apply and your grout spreader to spread evenly. Make sure you get it in all the gaps between the glass. After it is thickly and evenly coated, use the edge of the spreader to wipe off the excess on a paper towel. Do not reuse the excess. Wait for the grout to show a powdery film before sponging it off.

9. With a damp sponge held flat to the surface, gently wipe the top of the glass mosaic clean in a circular motion. Do not press too hard or the grout will come out. Rinse the dirty sponge between wipes. The object is to get the grout off the surface of the glass.

10. Allow the grout to cure, usually about 72 hours.

11. Do a second damp wipe after the grout is completely dry and scrub off any grout on the glass. You can grout a second time if you want to make the surface smooth and level. It's worth a second layer of grout because these tile edges are sharp, so you do not want the edges exposed.

Cutting glass into tiles.

Applying grout to the top of the trivet.

Spreading the sanded grout.

Smoothing the grout around the sides.

Sponging off excess grout.

Ceramic Slip Molds

BY GARTH JOHNSON

While it's admittedly time consuming, slip mold casting is fun and a perfect way to make a truly unique yet reproducible object. If you partner up with someone, at the end, you can each have your own set of molds because all the upfront work allows you to create multiples of the same object. This slip mold casting craftshop teaches you how to make a three-part teapot mold from a chocolate syrup bottle and a few second-hand teapots. I scour flea markets and thrift stores for old silver-plated teapots, and pull off the handles from them to make my molds. (You combine these pieces into one gorgeous object in the Bling Bling Teapot on page 156.) Once you learn the slip mold cast technique, you'll be able to make lots of other shapes for various projects.

You'll Need:

Empty dishwasher detergent or chocolate syrup bottle

Salvaged teapots

Set of cottle boards. (Most of us don't own a set of "cottle" boards, which make the frame of your mold. They consist of four ordinary boards (about 1/2" thick) with a piece of 1/2" square board screwed flush with one side.)

Masonite board

4 C-Clamps

Bag of #1 Pottery Plaster

Bag of clay

Murphy's Oil soap

1-2 gallon bucket

5-gallon bucket

Electric drill with mixer attachment

Stanley Shureform Shaver or rasp

Laying the bottle on the masonite board and embedding in clay.

Creating a box around the board with your cottle boards.

Pouring the plaster into the mold.

Pulling off the clay from the mold to create the second piece.

Two parts of the mold.

Keying the mold.

The three–part mold.

Splitting the mold.

Removing the bottle once the three sides of the mold are done.

MAKING IT

1. Analyze the object that you are about to mold—in this case, a chocolate syrup bottle. A plaster mold is inflexible so you can't have any "undercuts" on the chocolate syrup bottle. Undercuts are places where you would need to peel back the mold to get the object out. Imagine that the part of the mold that you are making must come away cleanly from the bottle. Use a sharpie marker to draw a line around the vertical middle of the bottle, where the mold will come apart. This is the seam of your mold. Check again for undercuts.

2. Lay your bottle on the Masonite board and surround it with clay. Embed the bottle halfway in the clay, with a plane of clay extending from the seams you have drawn. Extend the clay 1" from the widest point of the object. Ignore the bottom seam, as you will use the bottom cottle board to cover it. Now one half of your chocolate syrup bottle is surrounded on three sides by clay.

3. Create a box around the clay with the cottle boards. Use the C-clamps to secure them. Make a funnel of clay leading from the top of your object to the top cottle board. You will pour your ceramic slip in and out of this funnel.

4. Carefully smooth all of the clay down and seal the seams of the cottle boards with a coil of clay. This ensures no plaster will get between your cottle boards and your clay, which would make the mold sloppy looking.

5. Brush a thin layer of Murphy's Oil soap onto the surface of your bottle to prevent it from sticking to the mold.

6. Fill each of your buckets halfway with room-temperature water. Gradually sift plaster through the screen into your small bucket until a small island of dry plaster forms on top of the water. Allow the plaster to soak for five minutes. Do not disturb the bucket during this time.

7. With mixer attached to electric drill, mix the plaster until it begins to thicken. Avoid introducing too many air bubbles into the plaster. When you can make a small indentation in the surface of the wet plaster, it is ready to pour.

8. Soak the drill attachment in the big bucket of water so the plaster does not dry and stick to it.

9. Pour the plaster into your mold, making sure the plaster extends at least 1" above your object. Gently shake the board to dislodge any air bubbles caught in the plaster.

10. Pour a bit of water into your plaster bucket. Clean all of the plaster out of the bucket before it dries. Do NOT pour any plaster into your sink.

11. Let the plaster dry for about 30 minutes. Remove the cottle boards away, flip the mold over with the plaster side down, and remove all of the clay. Clamp a quarter or nickel into the drill and bore out a hole in each corner. This will create a negative and positive bump that will hold your mold together. Create the other side of the funnel from the top of the bottle for the second half of the teapot body mold. Cover the plaster and object with a thin layer of Murphy's Oil soap. Replace the cottle boards around the sides of the plaster and seal the corners with a coil of clay. Repeat plaster process.

12. After the second part of the mold has dried for 30 minutes, carefully pry the two parts of the mold apart. Make sure the bottle remains firmly in place.

13. Use the coin and drill to bore four holes in the corners of the bottom of the mold. Cover the bottom of the mold and bottle with Murphy's Oil soap. If you need to, use a knife or scraper to clean up

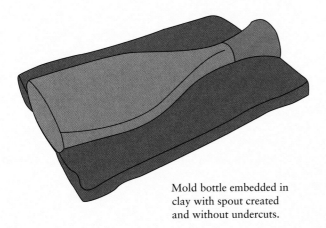

Mold bottle embedded in
clay with spout created
and without undercuts.

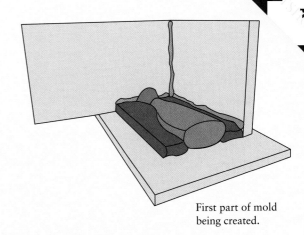

First part of mold
being created.

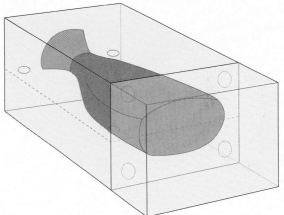

Bottle inside three-
piece mold.

the seams. Replace the cottle boards and repeat the plaster process.

14. After the plaster has dried for 30 minutes, carefully pry the three pieces of the mold apart and remove the object. If the object comes out neatly, you have done a good job finding the seams.

15. Once the mold has dried for at least one hour, clean it under running water. Use a scrub brush to rinse off all of the Murphy's Oil soap and clay. With a Shureform shaver or rasp, plane down the sharp edges of the mold.

16. Let the mold dry for three days. I put it in my gas oven (with the oven off—only the pilot light warming it) with the door cracked. Too much heat will make your mold brittle.

17. Make separate molds for your handle and spout using your old, scavenged teapots. The handles and spouts are molded like the teapot body, but only require two parts, rather than three. I create a "drain" on the spout mold to drain the excess slip from the bottom rather than pouring it out of the top. The spout is cast solid.

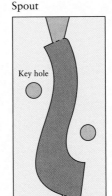

Spout

Key hole

Drain

Position of drains and
keys on the spout.

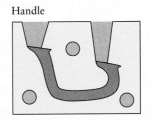

Handle

Position of the drains
and keys on the handle.

Bling Bling Teapot

BY GARTH JOHNSON

Face it. Anyone who got into pottery since 1990 did so because of the movie *Ghost*. When you're learning pottery, though, the loving arms of Patrick Swayze (or Demi Moore) aren't always wrapped around you. Although I can make a decent ashtray, I never really made it out of the bush leagues when it came to pottery. Fortunately, in ceramics, there are alternatives to manhandling the potter's wheel or painting little figurines at a hobby shop. Most ceramic objects in this world are made by slip casting, a process involving plaster molds and a liquid clay called slip. There are artists and craftspeople who make exquisite, delicate molds that are works of art in themselves. Unfortunately, I'm not one of those people. I make teapots out of simple slip casts of plastic bottles combined with handles and spouts taken from old silver-plated coffee pots. I don't really have a studio, so I'm fine with making plaster molds in my kitchen. The process really isn't very complicated. Even a caveman-simple plaster mold can produce excellent results. (See slip mold craftshop page 152.)

You'll Need:

Teapot molds (see Craftshop on slip mold casting, page 152 for making molds)

1 gallon commercial ceramic slip (available from ceramic hobby shops)

8 large rubber bands

Exacto or other brand utility knife

Small bag of clay

2 buckets

Plastic tarp

Ceramic glaze to match the temperature range of your slip (usually available at the ceramic studio or hobby shop you found to work in)

Ceramic gold luster

Rubbing alcohol

A respirator (available at hardware or home improvement stores and most art and craft supply stores) OR 1 premade teapot

Printable transfer paper (Lazertran) or other custom ceramic decals

Rhinestones (various kinds, sizes, a few handfuls)

24-hour epoxy glue

If you are really intrepid you can set up a home kiln, but this is quite an undertaking unless you do, or plan to do, quite a bit of ceramics. Otherwise, this project assumes you have access to a kiln. You may be able to strike up a deal with your ceramic studio, local hobby shop, or "paint your own pottery" business.

MAKING IT

MAKING THE TEAPOT

1. Go some place where you can make a mess. Even with a lot of newspaper laid down, inevitably, your slip will get on the floor. This is a good project for a backyard, a garage or some other studio like space. Assemble the molds for your teapot body, your handle, and your spout and secure together with large rubber bands. Put a bit of clay into the drain hole of your spout mold.

2. Put the slip into a bucket and pour the slip into your molds. Give them a few thumps to dislodge any air bubbles.

3. Let the slip sit in the spout mold for about 3 minutes, refilling as the level of the slip drops due to water evaporation. When the walls of the spout are thick enough, about 1/8" thick, remove the clay drain stopper on the bottom, and let the liquid slip drain back into the bucket. Let the slip sit in the teapot body mold for 10-15 minutes, refilling the slip as necessary and pouring out. Body should be about 1/8" thick. The handle mold is solid, so pour in more slip whenever you need it.

4. Allow the slip in all the molds to dry for at least 1 hour.

5. Remove the plaster molds, and you now have your teapot parts. Your molds may not work the first time, but don't fret! Try a few more times. If you have problems removing the mold, check the mold for undercuts (see Craftshop on page 152). If you have problems with the clay cracking, you are probably leaving the clay in the mold for too long. If you have problems with the clay breaking as you pull it out of the mold, you may be making it too thin or not leaving it in the mold long enough.

6. Let your teapot parts dry for another 30 minutes. At this point, you can wrap them tightly in plastic and come back to them later. With an Exacto knife, trim the excess clay from the seams and top of your pot.

7. Decide where you'd like to place your handle and spout, then cut a hole for the spout with the Exacto knife. Use some slip to adhere the handle and spout to the teapot body. Score the joining areas with your Exacto as well to ensure a proper seal.

Let your teapot dry. You may want to cover it in plastic to allow it to dry more slowly to avoid cracking. After the pot is bone-dry, you can use a sponge to smooth out any remaining seams or rough spots.

FIRING AND GLAZING

1. Bisque your pot to cone 04. Bisque firing stabilizes your pot and makes it ready for glazing.

2. Glaze your pot with whatever glaze you'd like to use. I like to use crackle glazes for the handle, and a white glaze for the body. (Glazes are generally done via a dipping method in a large bucket.) Fire the pot to the temperature indicated by your glaze. Use rubbing alcohol to remove any dust or smudges. Then apply gold luster in a thin coat to the handle and spout. Be careful to wear a respirator—luster is toxic. You can clean your brush in acetone. If you don't want to use ceramic luster, you may want to consider using a "gold" glaze, or even gold paint or leaf—but you will want to apply this after your final firing.

3. Give the pot its final firing; most gold luster matures at cone 018.

DECORATING YOUR TEAPOT

1. Make a design for your teapot, either on a computer, or by hand. You can collage images from magazines or draw by hand, then scan the final design. There are a few designs at SuperNaturale.com to get you started.

2. Print your design in reverse onto the Lazertran paper, then carefully cut out the design and soak it in lukewarm water until the decal starts to separate from the backing. Slide the decal onto your pot so the design faces the right way. Smooth out any bubbles trapped between the decal and the pot with a sponge. (Alternately, you can order decals that can be fired in the kiln at www.easyceramicdecals.com.)

3. Warm up the pot for about an hour at 150-degrees in your oven to dry out the decal. Gradually turn up the heat until you reach 400-degrees over the course of two hours.

4. Allow the pot to cool. When it is finished, the surface should be glossy and durable.

5. In a well-ventilated area and using epoxy, embellish the teapot with whatever objects you see fit—rhinestones, plastic jewels... real jewels... BLING BLING!

WOOD METAL

part 5

Wheelbarrow Fireplace

This is pretty much the easiest, cheapest way besides digging a hole to have a fire pit in your backyard. And best of all, it moves!

You'll Need:

An old metal wheelbarrow

12 bricks

Logs for your fire

A place to put the fireplace

MAKING IT

1. Find a safe place to have an open fire. Right next to the house is NOT a good place. On a highly flammable surface is not a good place. Think about those people who deep-fried their turkeys and set their patios on fire. I think about them all the time.

2. Roll your wheelbarrow to that nice safe spot.

3. Line the bottom of your wheelbarrow with bricks so that they touch. This provides a protective barrier between the fire and the heat conductive metal.

4. Build a fire.

5. Toast your marshmallows.

CRAFT MORE

❖ To make unusual colored flames in your new wheelbarrow fireplace, you can soak pinecones in a solution of water and a single chemical. Each chemical produces a different color: Copper sulfate makes green flames, potassium chloride makes purple, and plain old borax gives you a yellow-green. You can find potassium chloride in your supermarket because it's used as a salt substitute. Your drugstore or laundry section should have borax, and copper sulfate is found wherever swimming pool supplies are sold.

❖ Dissolve a half pound of one chemical in a plastic pail containing a gallon of water. Soak pine cones overnight. Dry thoroughly on newspapers and they're ready to burn brightly in a well-ventilated fireplace.

❖ All chemicals are potentially hazardous so keep in mind a few common sense rules: Wear rubber gloves and safety goggles when handling chemicals. Mix them outdoors but be careful not to spill them. Do not mix more than one chemical at a time. Keep chemicals away from children and pets. Store them in glass or plastic containers (not metal). Pay strict attention to any warnings listed on chemical labels.

Know Your Hardware

Tools—how intimidating the mere word sounds! Whether you're thinking of screamingly loud power tools from Home Depot or a garage workbench, tools seem like the turf of the manly, macho, and masculine. Fortunately for all tool-wielding mamas out there, chicks with chainsaws aren't doomed to be scantily clad on basement calendars. Take out your glue gun, screwdriver, and monkey wrench, and get ready for some hardcore craft.

TYPES OF TOOLS

Tools can insert and remove fasteners, cut, and measure. A hammer inserts and removes nails, working as a lever. A screwdriver pushes screws in by turning and applying pressure. Pliers are multipurpose and can pull out various kinds of fasteners. A wrench tightens and loosens bolts when turned. The highest-quality hammers, screwdrivers, pliers, and wrenches are made of steel, with rubber or acetate grips.

A glue gun shoots hot glue to work as an adhesive. A saw, made of steel, uses razor-sharp teeth to cut through wood. A knife, preferably stainless steel, uses a sharp blade to cut through plastic, paper, or fabric. Scissors work similarly to knives, using steel shears instead of a blade.

A ruler measures lines drawn and keeps them straight, while a tape measure is more useful for measuring long distances and curving or angled shapes. A level makes sure that any three-dimensional object is hung level or sitting level.

Quality tools can be expensive, but spending $15 on a handsaw that will break after two uses is not the greatest investment. Check out yard sales and garage sales for older but sturdy tools—age might even be a good thing, because the tool was made before our era of disposability. Scrub off rust and it's good as new, if slightly more battered. Online auctions may provide similar finds. You may be forced to spend some cash in search of the perfect tool, but in terms of durability and bang for the buck, it's worth it.

TYPES OF FASTENERS

Fasteners, usually made of steel, come in several varieties. Screws are a basic threaded fastener that requires wood with a corresponding groove for the screw to fit in. The number of a screw indicates the shaft diameter and the amount of screw heads per inch. Bolts are threaded like screws but require a nut at the other end to secure them. The nut can be tightened and loosened with a wrench. Often a washer will be used to cushion the fastened material from the nut. Nails come in various lengths and are used with a hammer to fasten wood. The length of a nail is traditionally measured by "penny weight," or how many used to cost a penny.

CRAFTSHOP

TOOLS

Hammer	Claw hammer	Forces in nails with head, removes with "claw" in back
	Ball-peen hammer	Used for metal-working
Screwdriver	Phillips	Matches Phillips-head screws
	Flat-blade	Matches slotted screw
	Electric	Various bits for different screws, electrically-powered
Pliers	Needle-nosed	Good for gripping in small spaces
Wrench (spanner)	Monkey wrench	Adjustable end for different bolts
	Socket wrench	Different sizes — sold as set
	Allen Wrench	Different sizes — sold as set
Glue gun	Glue gun, glue sticks	Electric-powered, uses hot glue to adhere surfaces
Saw	Chainsaw	Electric-powered, used for felling trees
	Handsaw	Hand-powered, cuts wood and plywood
Knife	Utility knife	Uses razor blade, cuts out patterns in most materials
	Swiss Army knife	Multi-purposed knife and other tools
Scissors	Regular scissors	Cuts straight with shearing motion
	Pinking shears	Serrated edges create patterns
Ruler	Ruler/straightedge	Measures and ensures straight line
	Tape measure	Measures long distances, bends for odd shapes
Level	Spirit level	Ensures centeredness, horizontal/vertical balance

FASTENERS

Screws (all wood screws)	Pan-head screw	Low disc for head
	Flat-head screw	Tapering inner edge, used for wood
	Slotted screw	Needs flat-blade screwdriver
	Phillips screw	Cross-shaped slot, requires Phillips-head screwdriver
Bolts	Hex lag bolt	Sharp point for working in woods
Nuts	Simple nut	Hexagonal nut, used with wrench
	Wing nut	"Wings" on either side, tightened by hand
Washers	Flat washer	Rests between nut and bolt
Nails	Wire nail	Most common type of nail
	Finishing nail	Smaller than wire nail, head hidden under surface
	Duplex nail	Temporary; two heads for easy removal

The Chelsea Bed

BY MEEGHAN TRUELOVE

OK, confession: after leaving my mother's house at the age of eighteen, I made it well into my adult life before I had another bed. Futons? Of course. I had plenty of futons. Futons and sleeping bags were part of my regular vocabulary—anything that could be folded up, tossed in cars, and flopped down on new floors. But I was afraid that a bed might somehow threaten my freedom. They seemed fussy and expensive and, most of all, permanent.

You'll Need:

WOOD
(for a queen size bed—80" x 60")

Platform: 3/4" plywood—make sure at least one side is sanded

I piece of 3/4" plywood 80" x 48"

I piece of 3/4" plywood 80" x 12"

Frame: 2" x 6" wood—get the least rough you can afford.

2 pieces of 2" x 6" cut to 80"

2 pieces of 2" x 6" cut to 57"

Keep in mind that a 2" x 6" is actually 1 1/2" x 5 1/2". These instructions have accounted for actual rather than stated dimensions of wood.

Crossbar: I piece of 2" x 6" cut to 77"

Legs: 2" x 6" wood—get the least rough you can afford

4 pieces of 2" x 6" cut to 35 1/2"

4 pieces of 2" x 6" cut to 30"

Hammer—if you're buying one, don't skimp. Get a proper big one, with a good rubber grip.

I box of 2 1/2" nails (If you have a power screwdriver, and you know how to use it, you can substitute screws for nails.)

Top: plywood is 3/4" thick

Frame: all are 2" thick and 6"wide

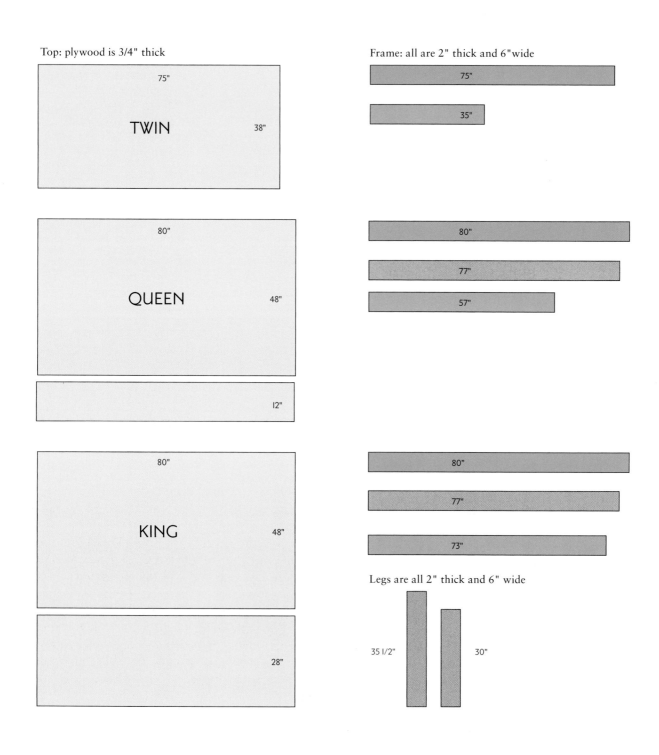

75"	
TWIN	38"

75"

35"

80"

QUEEN 48"

12"

80"

77"

57"

80"

KING 48"

28"

80"

77"

73"

Legs are all 2" thick and 6" wide

35 1/2"   30"

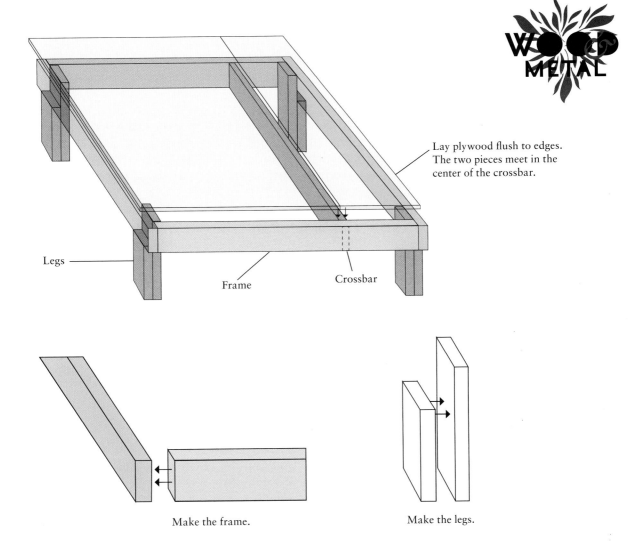

Lay plywood flush to edges. The two pieces meet in the center of the crossbar.

Legs

Frame

Crossbar

Make the frame.

Make the legs.

I hit bed-less rock-bottom when I broke up with a long-time, live-in lover and left him the most recent in our long line of futons. I found a new apartment and started sleeping on a camping mattress—not one of those cushy ones that simulate a decent bed, but an inches-thin mattress just wide enough for my body and just thick enough to keep my nose above the floor. I kept insisting to friends that this arrangement was comfortable enough, which it was, in a way. I'd slept on the mattress in foreign train stations and on back-woods camping trips, and using it after the breakup helped ease my hurt and confusion by making it all seem like one big adventure. But in truth I couldn't be bothered to get a new futon. I felt sore and raw, and thought that at any moment I might need to heed the urge

to flee. I continued using the camping mattress—for a year and a half.

A new lover entered my life and booked a ticket to come visit from afar. I was determined to honor this visit with a respectable place for romping and cuddling. No camping mattress, of course, but no fly-by-night futon, either. I needed a bed, and fast. A brilliant, orange-haired friend with unbounded creativity and a knack for coming to the rescue sketched out the plan of a bed she and a friend had designed and built. The design is basically a rectangle of 2" x 6"s with plywood board nailed on top. It consists of nothing but wood and nails (or screws). One person could make this bed, it's easier with two.

Now Chelsea is a fixer-upper, a do-it-yourself wonder gal with a staple gun in one hand and a spackle spatula in the other. Her design seemed fine, sure, but I protested that I wasn't going to be able to build it. I had no handy-woman experience and no confidence in my ability to make that bed. She insisted that I could. She explained the plan and explained it again. She gave me a rousing pep talk, full of all the confidence in me that I lacked in myself, and two days later my mom and I were in Home Depot, buying wood and getting it cut to size. (Unless you have a circular or table saw, get the wood cut for you where you buy it. All of the wood needed for the bed is cut from standard pieces that should be in stock at any lumberyard or home improvement store.)

By the end of the next afternoon, I had a bed. Chelsea's plan proved genius—just challenging enough to be really rewarding and just simple enough for me to completely understand.

The lover came to visit. The bed worked perfectly. But even more than being a love nest, my new bed became a safe haven, and I finally realized that what I'd been needing all along was a solid place from which to figure out where to go next.

MAKING IT

1. Make the frame. Lay the shorter pieces of the frame wood inside the longer pieces, with the 1 1/2" side up. Nail the four pieces together, using several nails at each joint. Build the bed against a wall if you can or get a friend to help by pushing against the rectangle like a brace so that you can nail the frame together without the planks moving all over the place.

2. Nestle the fifth plank (the crossbar) inside the bed frame, 1 1/2" side up, so that the left edge of the crossbar is 12 1/2" from the right edge of the frame. Check to make sure that the crossbar is in the right place by laying down (but not nailing in) one of the pieces of the platform (see page 169). The crossbar piece is going to run along the seam where the two pieces of plywood meet. When the position is good, remove the plywood and nail the crossbar in place.

3. Make the legs. Each leg is made of two pieces of wood, one of which is 5 1/2" shorter than the other. Lining up one end of each piece, nail the 5 1/2" sides of the legs together. The base of the finished legs (the end which is even) will be approximately 5 1/2" x 3". According to the cut list provided, the platform is about 3' off the ground, which means that with a 12" mattress, you will climb 4' to get into bed. If you don't need the storage, or if such a height doesn't make you feel like a princess, get shorter legs cut at the lumber yard. Reduce the length of the wood for the legs by equal amounts (no matter how tall you want the bed to be, one set of wood for the legs will need to be 5 1/2" longer than the other set). The legs can also be cut down after building the bed, by you'll need a saw.

4. Attach a leg to each corner of the frame. The longer piece of the uneven end of the leg pieces should rest on the floor and the shorter end should rest on the top of the frame. The bottom of the legs will stick straight up in the air. Use plenty of nails to secure in place.

5. Flip the bed over to stand on its legs. "It will wobble like a wet noodle," Chelsea said, and it does, but take heart, the next step will take care of that problem.

6. Attach the platform. Lay the plywood sheets on top of the rectangle so that they meet on the crossbar. Put the nicer side of the plywood, face up, to protect your mattress. Nail these platform pieces to the frame and crossbar. The bed will magically become strudier as you nail the plywood to the rectangle, and will have become rock solid by the time you slam in that last nail.

7. Flop a mattress on top. Voilà. You've got a bed. Add bedding and bodies. Sweet dreams.

CRAFT MORE

✤ If you increase the dimensions of the platform and the frame, you will have created a wooden shelf around the mattress. If you're not living in a shoebox, this can be a nice feature to use for books, tissue, or other necessary objects.

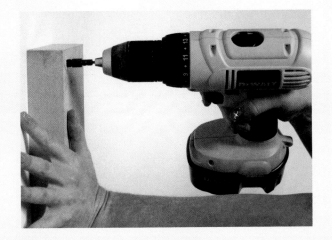

Woodworking

Not a carpenter? We'll fix that. This quick-and-easy guide covers types of wood and things you'll want to do to it. Check out the Know Your Hardware on page 164 for more on general tools like saws and hammers—stay here for sanders, oils, and varnish.

TYPES OF WOOD

Wood comes in three basic types. Hardwoods, like oak, maple, and rosewood, come from deciduous trees (you know, the ones whose leaves fall off for the winter). They're usually denser and heavier than their softwood cousins. Softwoods, such as pine, spruce, and cedar, are from coniferous trees, also known as evergreens—with needles instead of regular leaves. Plywood, which you'll probably be using, consists of manufactured panels in three or so layers of wood laid at 90-degree angles to each other. Plywood can be made of either spruce or the stronger birch. MDF, medium density fiberboard, is a composite made from compacted sawdust-like pieces and formaldehyde. It isn't very eco-friendly but doesn't need a lot of finishing. It is cheap, smooth-surfaced, and can be used in the same way as plywood. Veneer is a very thin sheet of wood that can be glued onto a less attractive core panel for appearance's sake. Veneers are often used on doors and cabinets, or anything else with a flat exposed surface. Lumber comes in two types, select and common, each with its own grades.

ECO WOODS AND COMPOSITES

Of course, there's an environmental angle on wood—not all timber is created equal in terms of impact on our ecosystems. The use of old-growth wood is the most damaging to the environment, since the ancient forests it's harvested from are destroyed and clear-cut to provide it. One alternative is to use bamboo, which is a grass, rather than a tree; it can be cut and grow back completely in five years. The display shelf on page 184 is made from Kirei board—an eco-composite comprised of sorghum stalks. Working with reclaimed wood, from buildings that have been deconstructed, is a great

Countersinking a screw is an effective way to keep your woodwork clean and sound. It makes the screw flush with the edge of your work. The pre-drilling helps prevent the wood from cracking when you put in the screw.

way to recycle high-quality timber. Some wood products are certified by the Forest Stewardship Council, which means that they're from sustainable forests, in which the removal of the trees isn't accompanied by general clear-cutting. The bonus for FSC-certified products is that they're the same wood you'd be using anyway—the source is just environmentally friendly.

Composites are also ecologically sound, since they use up scraps of timber that would normally be thrown away. There's an eco-friendly material for any wood project you can imagine.

MAKING HOLES

If you want to join two pieces of wood together you need to make a hole and insert a nail or screw into it. Before you insert a screw, pre-drill the hole with an electric drill and countersink bit. Pre-drilling prevents the wood from cracking when you put in the screw. Always pre-drill a hole smaller than your screw. A countersink is a special drill bit that is wider on the top. Countersinking produces a taper or cone shape surface at the entrance of a hole so that the head of your flat head screw sits flush with the surface of your wood. Countersink bits come in a variety of widths that match screw widths.

HAND SANDING

Sanding wood is essential to ensure an attractive, smooth finish. You don't want to get splinters every time you touch your project. Sandpaper comes in several types, including aluminum oxide and garnet. Aluminum oxide sands faster and lasts longer, but its finish is less smooth. Garnet sandpaper wears out quickly, but has a very smooth finish, making it ideal for the last round of sanding. Whichever type you're using, make sure it's open-coat rather than closed-coat, which allows space for dust and makes the sandpaper last longer.

You have to put your sandpaper on something, and your main options are a sanding block or a sanding machine. To make a sanding block, simply wrap sandpaper around a piece of flat wood in whatever size works best for your project—usually about palm-sized—and hold on tight. A sanding machine works faster, but is more expensive ($50 to $100) and uses up more sandpaper. A palm-grip random orbit sander is small but gets the job done. Use it with fine sandpaper.

For the actual process, sand along the grain for the best looks. It is important that you sand your piece evenly. Your end product will only look as good as your sanding. Sand your wood with at least two different "grit levels" of sandpaper, preferably using coarse, medium, and fine. Beginning with the coarsest, sand thoroughly with each type before you move on to the next—skipping a grit level could take a lot longer, as well as diminish your project's good looks.

The next and final step is finishing. There are many finishing options but what follows are general guidelines for the simplest, most environmentally sensitive and amateur friendly. We finish wood for beauty, durability and to mitigate something called water vapor exchange. Your wood was once a living material and it still contracts and expands in response to humidity. If you live in an environment with humidity extremes, New England for instance, this may be a concern. A traditional way to finish wood is to oil and then wax it. A very durable finish is varnish. Be sure to follow the directions of your finish.

OIL

Oil adds a satiny finish to your project and helps resist moisture, heat, and other furniture demons. It is less protective overall than varnish, though easier to apply. Many kinds of oil work well. If you are making a salad bowl or cutting board you would want to use a food safe mineral oil. For furniture you could use a "true" oil (such as polymerized tung or linseed), or something called an "oil" or "oil finish"—such as Danish oil, teak oil or tung finish—this is actually an oil-thinner or an oil-varnish mix and provides a more durable, quicker curing finish.

For application of Danish or teak oil, first remove the dust from your sanding. Apply an even coat with a soft cotton cloth. Be careful not to leave any pools of oil and wipe away any drip lines that may occur on the edges of the work. Leave it alone to cure, usually for at least eight hours. Rub it with a soft cotton cloth to get rid of the extra oil.

Apply a second coat more sparingly, then let it cure again and rub again. When do you stop? Around two or three coats, or when water dripped onto your wood rolls off the surface instead of being absorbed.

Wax is an excellent way to "finish" this finish. Air-dry your oil rags before throwing them out to prevent off gassing.

WAX

Wax is one of the most common methods of finishing wood, as well as the lightest way. High quality wood furniture wax, available at specialty stores, online or through catalogs, is actually a combination of carnauba, beeswax, synthetic, and vegetable waxes.

The texture is paste-like and you need to apply two or three light coats. If you are applying this over an oil finish, very lightly, use some steel wool to sand your finish so that the wax will adhere to the surface. Wait at least four hours before applying another coat. After the wax has dried, buff with a soft cotton rag. You only have to reapply wax every few years, unless you're unusually hard on your furniture.

VARNISH

Varnish will encase your wood in an impenetrable layer of urethane and therefore does a better job protecting wood than these other methods, but it's more labor-intensive to apply. Most varnishes are toxic as well and should only be applied in a well-ventilated area. Bear in mind that water-based varnish is non-toxic, the safest for the environment and easiest in terms of clean-up. Varnish comes with various pigments and styles of finish (matte, gloss, eggshell) so choose the look you like. Take the easy route, unless you have something specific in mind. The easiest kind of varnish to apply is wipe-on varnish, which may also contain oil. It has a gel-like consistency and can be applied with a soft cotton cloth and built up in many layers. Once a coat is dry, remove any dust specks with 240-grit sandpaper. This will also help the next layer adhere and is called "keying." Apply two or three total coats, or more, depending on the finish you desire, allowing drying time in between coats.

Embroidered Screen Door

BY JENNY HART

One day I saw a post on a craft website by a woman who mentioned that when she was little, her mother embroidered the screen door. That was all she said about it, but I was immediately interested and wanted to know more. How did she do it? Where did she get the idea? What was the design? Alas, these questions remained unanswered.

You'll Need:

Screen door (you can make your own door using standard sized, screen-door rolls)

Self-sticking tear-away stabilizer

Fluorescent embroidery floss

Tapestry needle

Scissors

Brush-on adhesive (clear nail polish, clear-drying acrylic gloss, Elmer's glue)

Spray sealant or varnish (optional)

Black lightbulb (check what type your porch fixture requires)

All I know is that Carol Clontz embroidered her screen door many years ago, and now you can too. It's not cozy, snuggled-in-an-armchair embroidery. You'll actually be embroidering on a metal screen!

It's really no different than any other kind of weave you stitch on. Your needle doesn't have to pass through each and every little square. In fact, you'll find you can work on this surface rather easily. The trick is in the setup and getting the right prep work done. But this project has enormous potential if you're willing to make the little extra effort.

The design is simple, and I hope this will lend inspiration for other ways to stitch this previously un-embroidered territory.

MAKING IT

1. Photocopy the designs from page 178.

2. Cut a piece from a roll of self-sticking stabilizer large enough to cover the entire design. Lay the stabilizer over the design, rough side up. The stabilizer is light enough that you should have no problem seeing the design through the stabilizer. Trace the design onto your stabilizer with a pen or marker.

3. Remove the backing from the stabilizer and lay it on the front of the screen where you want to place the design. The tack of the adhesive is light enough that you will be able to peel it away if you want to reposition the design.

Once you're happy with the placement, press the stabilizer against the screen lightly with your hand throughout to really secure it in place. You're ready to start stitching!

4. Cut a 24" length of floss from the skein. Double the length of floss (bring both ends together) and

thread your tapestry needle with both ends of the length. Keep all strands aligned. You'll only need 1" or 2" to pass through the eye (don't pull the floss all the way through). The remaining loop is your working tail. Do not knot it.

5. Now anchor the floss to the screen. Begin by entering the needle through the front of the screen and stop short of pulling the loop all the way through. In the direction of your pattern, come up next to the loop (use the next square), passing the needle through the loop and tightening.

Continue in the direction of your pattern and work your choice of any embroidery stitch. At each endpoint, tie a double knot.

Due to the transparent nature of the screen, you won't be able to take jump stitches across to the next section you'd like to stitch. Instead, cut your floss and secure a knot at each endpoint in the design. Leave a longer tail than usual. You will cut it after the next step.

6. When you're done embroidering your design, remove the stabilizer carefully. Try to avoid pulling the end knots through. I went back over the end points and tightened up the knots (that's why you want to leave extra tail). Apply your brush-on adhesive (wood glue or clear nail polish) to the knots. Let dry, and then snip away extra tail.

Varnishing the embroidery is optional. Use either a spray sealant (available at most art supply stores) or brush the stitches sparingly with a clear-drying acrylic gloss or a clear-drying adhesive. Just be sure to do this AFTER you've removed the stabilizer!

Chain Stitch
Bring thread or embroidery floss up through fabric from wrong side to right side. Make a tiny loop and insert the needle back where it just came out, but do not pull the loop through. Leave the little loop of thread on top, while reinserting the needle back up through fabric and inside this loop, or stitch. This keeps the loop from pulling through and makes a little chain on the right side of your fabric. If you repeat this pattern, you'll form a chain of stitches.

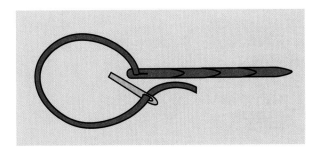

Split Stitch
Another continuous stitch, the split stitch is used in embroidery similarly to the chain stitch. You work it by literally making a stitch, and the bringing the needle up for the next stitch right through the middle of the previous stitch—"splitting" the thread or floss. The shorter your stitches, the nicer this looks and the easier it is to sew.

Pattern approximately 1/2 actual size.

SHOWCASE

Upholstered Tree Stumps: For a number of years I would happen upon a mysteriously upholstered tree stump and wonder about the maker. Eventually I met the woman behind these stumps. Madelon Galland told me she wants to draw attention to the things we overlook in a way that is both magical and yet totally down to earth.

Rice Table

BY DOUG LLOYD

My parents always gave me one "big" present for Christmas. One year a Hot Wheels track, another a bike, the next Atari. Every year the thing I truly desired sprang, fully assembled and ready to use, from my dreams. It was a miracle of childhood. Learning, as I grew older, that my Dad spent many a sleepless night pulling his hair out over poorly designed instructions made the miracle all the better. Well, now it's my turn to divine and manifest my child's holiday dreams. And who really cares about my hair, look how cute she is.

You'll Need:

I sheet of 3/4" plywood, 48" x 48" (to make the box)

4 pieces of 2" x 2" wood, each 16" long (for the legs, actual size is I 1/2" x I 1/2")

2 pieces of 2" x 2" wood, 48" long (for support, actual size is I 1/2" x I 1/2")

Handsaw

Circular saw (hand or table)

Drill

Small and large drill bits

Counter sink (optional)

Phillips-head screws, small and large

Phillips-head bit

80-, 100- and 240- grit sandpaper

Primer and paint or other sealant

Paintbrushes

80 pounds long grain white rice

A rice table is a sand box for the house. Rice is easier to clean up than sand, is edible, and doesn't stick to babies. I first saw a homebrew rice table at my good friends David and Lela's. My daughter's joy playing with their kids' table inspired me to make one for our home. The one shown here was made from scrap materials I had lying around. In other words, the design of the table was determined by what I had and not a desire to make something perfect. I also designed it relative to my daughter's height (she's tall), where I planned to put it (the finished table filled with rice is too heavy to easily move around), and to fit within the feel of our house. If you don't have the time to construct a full-on table, no worries, just put a couple bags of rice in a cardboard box. If you do have the time, here's how I did it.

MAKING IT

1. Cutting the pieces: Cut the 48" x 48" plywood sheet in half to make two 24" x 48" sheets. Cut one of these length-wise twice to make three 8" x 48" sheets. Put two of these aside (they will form the front and back sides of the box) and cut the third in half across the width to make two 8" x 24" sheets (these will form the right and left sides of the box). Now, take the other 24" x 48" sheet and cut 1 1/2" off the length to make it 46 1/2" x 24" (this will form the bottom of the box). With the handsaw, cut a 1 1/2" x 1 1/2" square from each corner (this is where the legs will go).

Box sides: Pre-drill a hole in each corner of the front and back pieces. Corner the holes 1" from each edge. Pre-drill a hole in each corner of the right and left side pieces. Corner the holes 2" from the edge on side's width and 1/2" from the edge on the side's length.

2. Box bottom: Pre-drill a row of three evenly spaced holes, 2 1/4" from each edge of the bottom's length.

3. Supports: Pre-drill a hole 1 1/2" from each end of the two supports. If you like, counter sinking the holes will give the table a more finished look.

4. Attach the legs to the sides: Attach two legs to the right side of the box and two legs to left side of the box. Do this by aligning a leg's face flush to the edge of a box side's length, and the leg's end flush with the edge of the box side's width. Attach each leg with two screws through the pre-drilled holes. Attach two legs to the same face of the right side and two legs to the same face of the left side of the box. Make sure the ends of the legs are flush with the same edge of the box sides.

5. Attach the front and back to the legs: Now, attach the front and back pieces. Position the edge of the box front's length so it overlaps with the edge of the box side's length. The front's edge should be flush with the side's face. Also, make sure the ends of the legs are flush with the edge of the side's length. Attach each leg with two screws through the pre-drilled holes. Attach all four legs to form the box.

6. Attach the support: Turn the box upside down so the legs stick up in the air. Lay the supports across the length of the box so they butt up against the legs' inside faces. Attach with screws through the support's holes into the legs.

7. Attach the bottom: Flip the box over and place the bottom in the box so it rests on the supports. Attach with screws through the bottom's holes into the supports.

8. Sand and seal: Since this is for a child make sure to sand off any rough or sharp edges and remove any dust. If you like, you can prime and paint or otherwise seal the wood.

9. Fill it with rice: Put the box where you want it and fill with rice. The box I made holds a good 80 pounds. I found long grain white rice works well and is affordable, but you could fill it with anything.

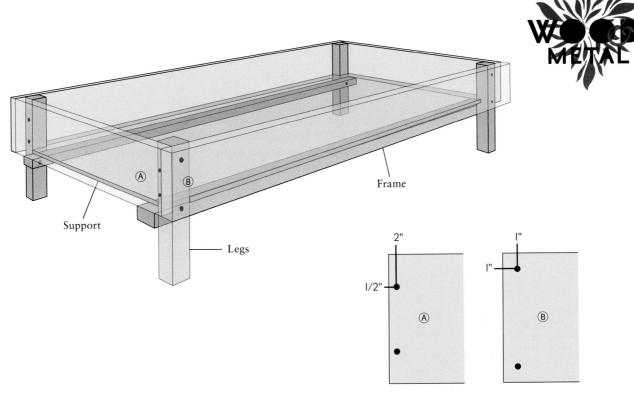

Frame

Support

Legs

2"

1/2"

Ⓐ

1"

1"

Ⓑ

Detail of countersink holes

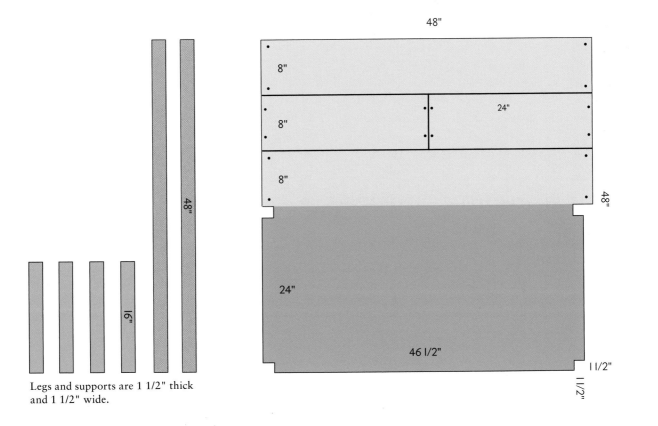

48"

8"

8"

24"

8"

24"

48"

46 1/2"

1 1/2"

1 1/2"

48"

16"

Legs and supports are 1 1/2" thick
and 1 1/2" wide.

W⬤⬤D
METAL

Lighted Display Shelf

by Susan Barber

I made this illuminated shelf in school, under the intensely helpful supervision of the Cooper Union wood shop staff. It originally held glass jars of sea water, with the lights out you could watch little organisms scurry about their business. Eventually the water got stinky, the jars now hold Q-tips in my bathroom, and the shelf has been home to most imaginable forms of foliage, correspondence, and knick-knackery: plastic animals, avocado pits in hopes of sprouting, cut flowers, potted plants, porcelain animals, love notes, post-it notes, sugar sculptures, liquor bottles, kites, origami… basically anything looks good when lit dramatically from below.

You'll Need:

Table saw with a left-tilting arbor

27" x 36" section of 20 mm Kirei board from Bettencourt Green Building Supplies

Chop or hand saw

White electrical tape

Wood glue

Corner brackets

1/2" finishing screws

Electric drill

16 watt, 20 1/2" self-mounting fluorescent light kit (called an "under counter light")

Wall mounting screws

8 11/16" x 27" piece of 1/8" frosted Plexiglas

Some pretty things to put on top when you're done

An end plug

Wire Cutters

27" by 36" of 20mm Kirei board

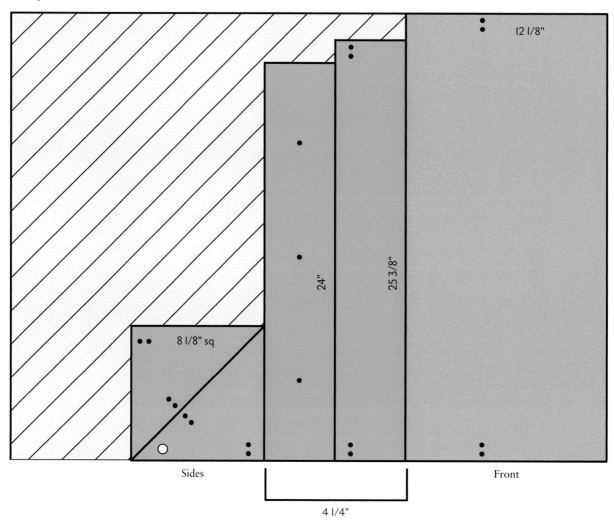

12 1/8"

8 1/8" sq

24"

25 3/8"

Sides

4 1/4"

Front

8 11/16" by 27" of 1/8" frosted Plexiglas

Top

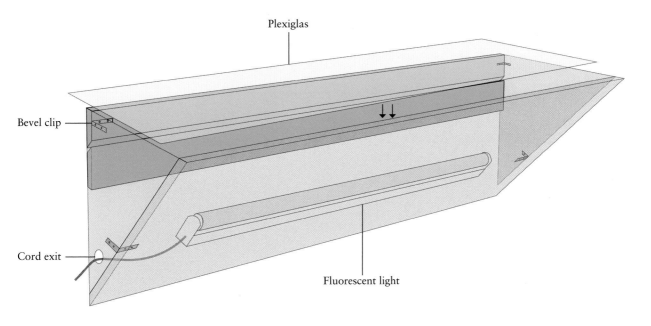

Plexiglas

Bevel clip

Cord exit

Fluorescent light

MAKING IT

1. Set the blade of the table saw to 45-degrees, set the fence to 12 1/4" and make a cut along the 27" length of the Kirei board.

2. Turn the piece you just cut around and make the same exact cut on the opposite edge. This will be the face of the shelf. (See figure A on next page.)

3. Lower the blade (still set at 45-degrees) to half the thickness of the material (10mm). Set the fence to 12". Make a cut along the top of the face of the shelf. (See figure B.) The notch you have just cut is for the Plexiglas to sit in. Set this piece aside.

4. Set the blade to 90-degrees. Set the fence to 4 1/4". Make a cut along the 27" length of the Kirei board. This is the wall mount, called a bevel clip.

5. Set the blade to 45-degrees and rip through the middle of the wall mount. One of these halves will attach to the shelf and the other to the wall. (See diagram C.)

6. Using a chop saw or a hand saw, cut one of these pieces down to 25 3/8". This is the piece that will attach to the shelf. Cut the other down to 24" for the piece that will attach to the wall. (See figure C.)

7. You now make two equilateral triangles, the sides of the shelf. Cut an 8 1/8" x 8 1/8" square from the remainder of your Kirei board. Then make a jig to cut on a diagonal through the middle of this square. (See figure D and detail D). This should leave you with two 7 15/16" triangles.

8. Now you are ready to assemble your shelf. You should have a total of five pieces.

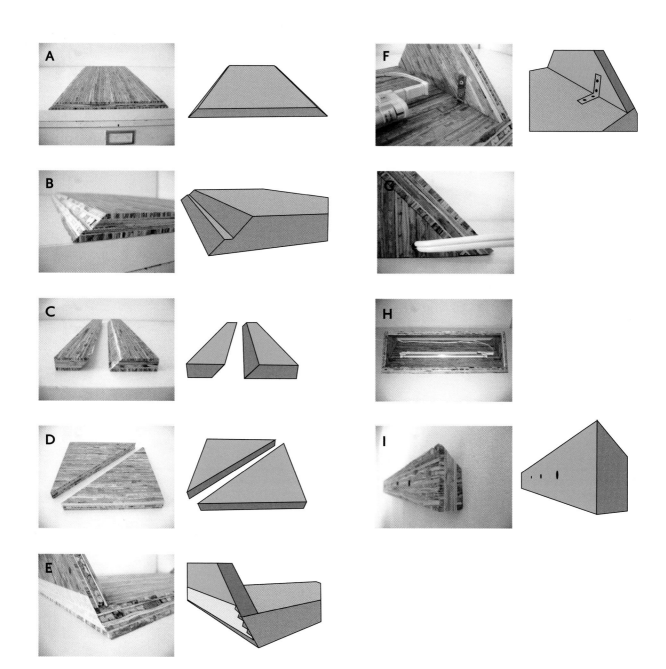

9. Using a pencil, mark each joint. (See figure E). Tape all the joints of the shelf together with white electrical tape. Then open one joint, lay everything out flat, and glue the pieces together with wood glue, one at a time. If the tape is tight enough it acts as a clamp. Let dry 24 to 48 hours.

10. When the glue is completely dry, remove the tape. Attach the corner brackets to the inside of each joint for extra strength. (See figure F.)

11. Drill a 1/4" hole in one side of the shelf. This is where the cord will exit. (See figure G.)

12. Mount the light on the inside of the face of the shelf. (See figure H.) Cut the plug off the cord. Feed the cord through the hole. Clip the end plug onto the cord.

13. Attach the wall half of the mounting unit to the wall. If you want to put heavy things on your shelf, be sure to either find the studs in the wall or use heavy-duty screw anchors. (See figure I.)

14. Hang the shelf on the wall mount and drop the Plexiglas in place. Arrange your lovely objects. Plug in the extension cord. Enjoy.

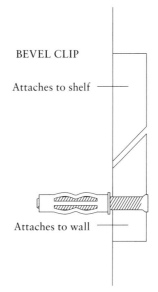

BEVEL CLIP

Attaches to shelf

Attaches to wall

Diagram of figure C

JIG

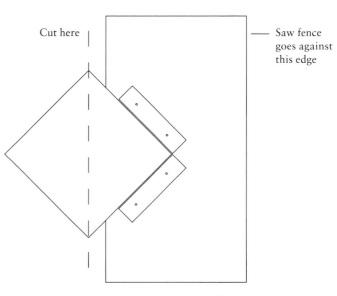

Cut here

Saw fence goes against this edge

Detail D

LOST & FOUND

part 6

Moss Graffiti

BY BRETT WEBB

The idea of growing plants as graffiti has been floating around in my head for awhile. When I was a more actively rebellious graffiti writer in L.A., I often talked and thought about guerilla farming. I imagined walking the streets of South Central, à la Johnny Appleseed, and planting sunflowers and tomatoes where buildings were burned down in the riots.

You'll Need:

Several clumps garden moss

I can of beer OR I cup of yogurt (test to see which works better in your location)

1/2 teaspoon sugar

I quart plastic container with lid

Blender

Paintbrush

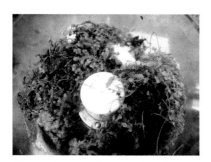

Moss recipe ingredients ready to be blended.

Drawing design for graffiti pattern.

Applying moss mixture.

In high school I visited the Black Hills and saw Mount Rushmore. I was so angry about it; it disgusted me. I didn't understand how the permanent defacing of a natural wonder could be a national monument, while my temporary markings on a manmade surface could land me in jail. It seemed obvious, to me, that the mountain should be beyond reproach, something that no man has the right to alter. I understood the impulse of wanting to interact with and manipulate nature, but I didn't understand the destructive nature of Mount Rushmore.

I like the idea of man affecting nature in a way that isn't harmful, but is playful and interactive. The growing should be outdoors and should be akin to graffiti found in the city. It should bring about the same wonder and excitement as when you find a fresh mural hiding in an alley or along a tunnel. It reminds me of a stack of rocks that you happen across on a trail or on the beach. The rocks make you wonder about the person who put them there. They are interesting visually, but are harmless to their surroundings. I hope that others can experience the sort of excitement that this project brings me.

MAKING IT

1. Gather several clumps of moss (moss can usually be found in moist, shady places, including city sidewalk cracks) and crumble them into a blender.

2. Add the beer or yogurt and sugar and blend just long enough to create a smooth, creamy consistency. Pour the mixture into a plastic container.

3. Find a suitable damp and shady wall on to which you can apply your moss milkshake. Paint your chosen design onto the wall (either free-hand or using a stencil).

4. Try to return to the area over the following weeks to ensure that the mixture is kept moist. Soon the bits of blended moss should begin to grow into a whole rooted plant—maintaining your chosen design before eventually colonizing the whole area.

(Recipe and concept courtesy Helen Nodding, London-based artist and provocateur. Visit her website storiesfromspace.co.uk to see examples of moss graffiti and many other genius ideas.)

Thrift Store Finds

BY CAROLINE HUTH

Every time I go to a thrift store, I seem to look at the same stuff. Broken-in khakis, vintage sweaters, plates that match the pattern I've been collecting for years. But I always forget to look at other stuff, stuff that you can actually "do something" with.

BOOKS

The other day I found, crammed between a textbook called *C++ for Professionals* and a syrupy looking novel called *Love's Wicked Ways*, a slim paperback entitled *Easy Sew-Ups and Appliqués*. Apparently somebody thought sewing was no longer hip. Shame on them.

TINS

Inevitably at most any thrift store there will be an entire shelf of ugly Christmas cookie tins. Why is this a good thing? Because tins make great shrines. Why make a shrine? Why not! Idolize photos of your cats, your boyfriend (or ex!) or whatever you feel deserves worship. I made a shrine to the almighty pistachio. The tin is covered in shell halves and when you open it, the inside has a single, perfect nut up on a little pedestal with birthday candles around it. I light them when I feel hungry. Tins are also great for homemade cookies or other treats. Cut a slit in them and make a kleenex dispenser (fold over sharp edges!). Spray-paint, decoupage, embellish them, whatever moves you. Just remember to use glue that'll stick to metal.

COFFEE TABLES

The greatest coffee tables come from thrift stores. And sometimes, they come in the shape of beat up suitcases or trunks or old tables that need their legs cut down. (See page 208.) My parents have a little coffee table that once was an antique sewing machine table. Those little side drawers are great for their four remote controls.

NECKTIES

Make them into skirts (okay, this is a little passé), quilts (this is not!), backpacks, potholders, or whatever. Just buy the cool ones, not polyester ties with stains on them.

RECORD ALBUMS

These have so many uses, I don't even know where to start. Decorate your walls with old vinyl. Hang them up as room dividers. Heat them up and make bowls. Use the jackets for book covers, folders, cards, postcards, framed art, CD holders, decoupage, or shower curtains. Darn, these things are useful.

Message Board

BY ANNA RADDATZ

When I moved into a new apartment with a lot of wall space, I went to the local liquor store where the salesman was thrilled to fork over as many boxes as I wanted, which were great for moving books, etc. After unpacking, I was left with trillions of little liquor/wine boxes. Throw them away? Heck no! If you are like me, over the years you have acquired many photos, postcards, and other little pictures that should be on display, but which don't each deserve their own frame. The obvious solution is a bulletin board, but a little bulletin board costs a lot of money (especially after paying a broker's fee). So instead I simply took those free boxes and made them into display boards.

You'll Need:

2 or 3 same-size corrugated cardboard boxes

2 yards of fabric, your choice

Packing tape

Scissors or Exacto knife

Stapler (with releasable hinge)

Nails

Hammer

Thumbtacks

The great things about this project are: 1) the materials are practically free; 2) your display board can be any color, shape, or size you desire or require; 3) it takes very little time to accomplish; and 4) it looks really chic—much sexier than a regular cork bulletin board.

Any kind of corrugated cardboard box will work, but for the shape I made, liquor/wine boxes were perfect. Make sure they are all the same size—different brands sometimes come in slightly different sized boxes. I also used a couple yards of muslin, which I had gotten on sale. You could even use several different fabrics to create a stripey effect.

MAKING IT

1. With either scissors or an Exacto knife, cut the boxes open by slicing down one side so that each box lays open flat.

2. Cut off all the flaps.

3. Layer the cardboard. You can either use three layers of box (with flaps cut off); or (if you're like me and hate to throw anything away) use two layers of box, plus one layer of the cut-off flaps which are taped together along their long edges so that they combine to form the same length.

4. Tape layers together with packing tape. If one of your layers consists of taped-together flaps, put that one in the middle. Run the tape around all four edges. Make sure that one of the outer sides is blank, without text or image; otherwise, the image may show through the fabric.

5. Lay fabric right-side-down on floor/table. Place cardboard blank-side-down on top of fabric. There should be a couple inches of extra fabric surrounding the edges.

6. Pull the edges of the fabric up onto the cardboard and staple it down in intervals of a few inches. You will need a stapler that can swing open so you can push it down directly onto the fabric/board.

7. Place your brand new display board against the wall and decide where you want it to be. While holding it there, mark on the wall with a pencil: two dots underneath right at the edge (one near each end), and one dot in the middle on the top (or two, one at either end, if you're really into hammering).

8. Take the display board down, and hammer in the bottom edge nails, with the nails aiming down, leaving about a centimeter sticking out of the wall. Place the display board on top of the nails, then hammer in the top nail(s), making sure that the head of the nail bends down over the front of the display board a bit to hold it in place.

9. Ta Da! Now you can attach stuff to it with thumbtacks (I like the flat, silver ones).

CRAFT MORE

✤ Make the board any size or shape, and cover with any fabric. They're so easy and cheap to make, you can make lots of them, and use them for all kinds of things.

✤ Wrap ribbon around the finished board and tuck in pictures, postcards, cards, etc.

✤ Pin different fabric or paper backgrounds to the front of the same board to change with the seasons or your moods. Cover with a holiday-ish fabric and use as a display for holiday cards—or cover with a plain fabric and use for different holidays year-round.

✤ Ooh, thumbtacks that match the fabric...

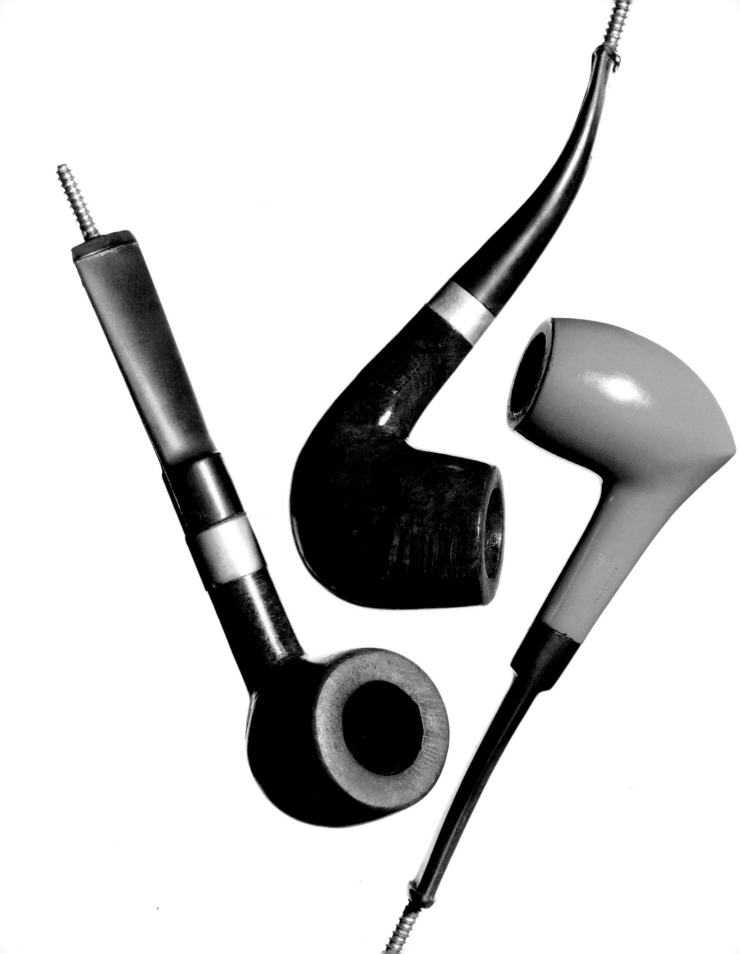

Magritte Pipes Candleholder

or Ceci n'est pas une luminaire

BY SCOTT BODENNER

A long time ago I had a boyfriend named Jody. He is a talented sculptor who likes to glorify the mundane and loves the French cultural theorist Derrida. While we were dating he had the original of this project in his home. I still treasure the memory of this fragile and surreal object. I suppose I should also mention that the name of the candle holder is an homage to the Belgian surrealist artist Rene Magritte. One of his paintings is of a pipe with the sentence "Ceci n'est pas une pipe."

You'll Need:

Vintage pipes, as many as you want to make holders. If you don't have ready access to these from estate sales or your uncle, eBay is calling you. The mouth pieces of pipes are fragile. Get a couple of extra pipes in case one or even two break. Look for pipes with bowls that are fairly perpendicular to the stems.

I two-sided screw per pipe, available at most hardware stores. Get a selection of small ones to fit the mouth piece holes in the pipe just in case. They are cheap, go ahead and treat yourself.

Two part liquid epoxy for metal and plastic

A drill

Graduated drill bits

MAKING IT

1. Hold the mouthpiece of the pipe down on the table with your palm to keep it steady.

2. Treat the hole of the mouth piece as if it is a pre-drilled hole for your two-sided screw. You will now enlarge this whole slightly by drilling into it. Move slowly while drilling—applying pressure and then removing the turning bit from the holes so the excess material can be expelled and there is not too much stress on the mouthpiece. Start with a drill bit that is just a little larger than the hole of the mouthpiece and go successively larger until one end of your screw will fit in the mouth piece hole.

3. Mix up a little blob of the epoxy and twist the two-sided screw into it. Insert the epoxied end into the pipe so that the same length is in the mouthpiece as is out of it. Remove any excess epoxy with a rag.

4. If you have broken through the mouthpiece or a bit of it has broken off, fill the gap or replace the part with the epoxy.

5. Let the epoxy cure even longer than the instructions say, at least overnight.

6. Find a stud in your wall and pre-drill it to the size of your two-sided screw. Take a regular screw the same size and work it into the hole so that the threads are in place in the stud.

7. Now carefully screw the two-sided screw sticking out of pipe mouthpiece into the wall.

8. Insert candle into the bowl where you would put the tobacco. You will probably want to use a shorter candle so as not to put too much weight on the pipe. When inserting the candle be very very gentle—the price for this surrealism is fragility.

Noney Money: Obadiah Eelcut invented this currency for bartering goods and services. Noney bills feature Rhode Island residents with their favorite bird, fruit, or vegetable. A few years ago, Obadiah cast a few hundred Noney notes into circulation. I am not kidding. Be on the lookout.

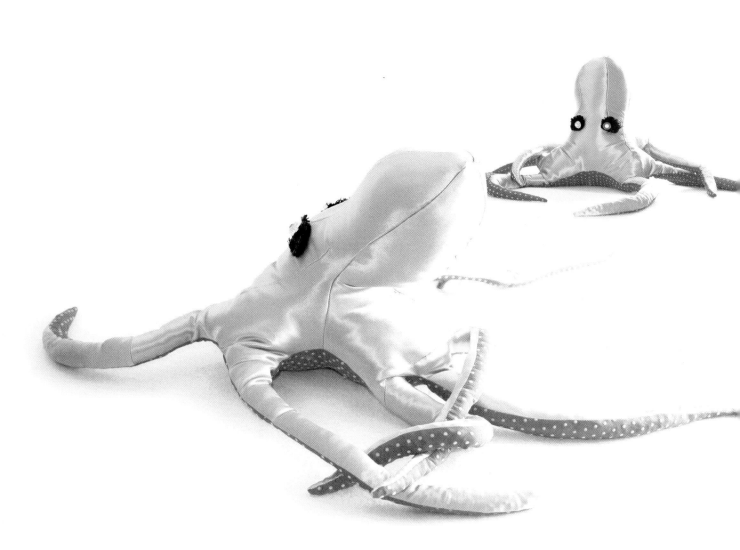

Soft Octopus

BY PEARCE WILLIAMS

I fell in love with fabric when I was 16 years old, learned to sew, and haven't stopped yet. I started making clothes for myself, because I didn't like the way store-bought clothes fit. Over the years, I've accumulated a frightening mass of gorgeous fabric, and being the kind of girl who doesn't like to throw out her scraps, I started sewing puppets and stuffed animals for my nieces out of the leftover material… sassy birds, lumpy dogs, melancholy elephants, greedy reptiles, and a few unidentifiables. The octopus is one of my most favorites.

You'll Need:

1 1/2 yards of fabric for the top side of the octopus (I like satin, or something with a little bit of a sheen to it)

1 yard of contrasting fabric for the underside (I've used a flocked polka dotted cotton here)

Scissors

Needle

Sewing thread

Straight pins

Small bit of wool or felt for the eyelids (wool is great because you can fray the edges)

2 buttons for eyes

1 bag of polyester stuffing

1 bag of dried beans

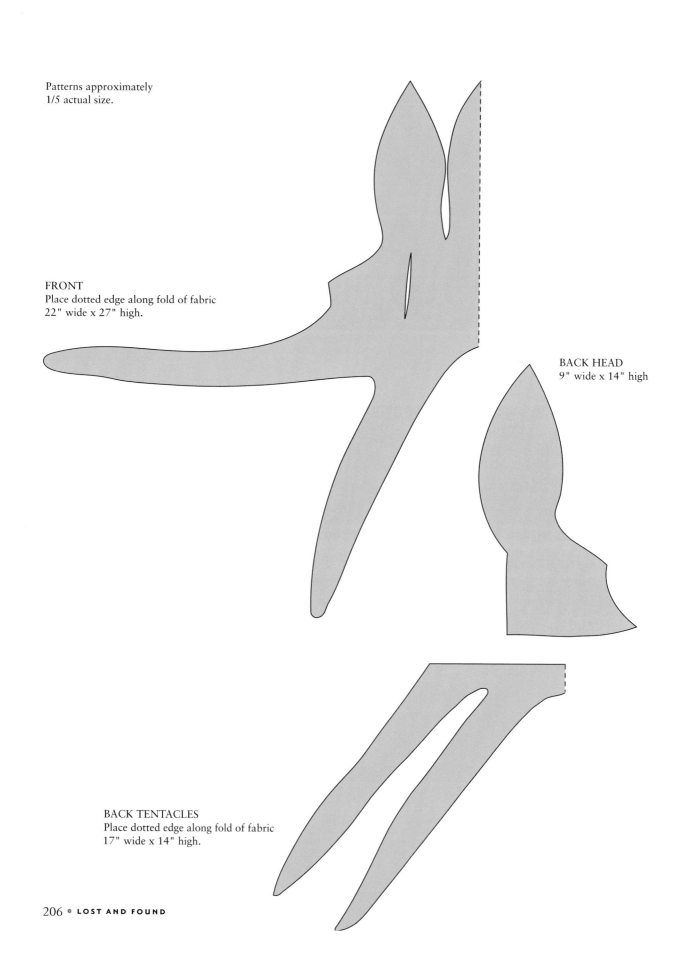

Patterns approximately
1/5 actual size.

FRONT
Place dotted edge along fold of fabric
22" wide x 27" high.

BACK HEAD
9" wide x 14" high

BACK TENTACLES
Place dotted edge along fold of fabric
17" wide x 14" high.

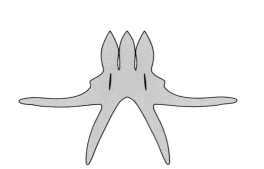

Front pattern laid out.

Sew on eyes.

Cut two back head pieces.

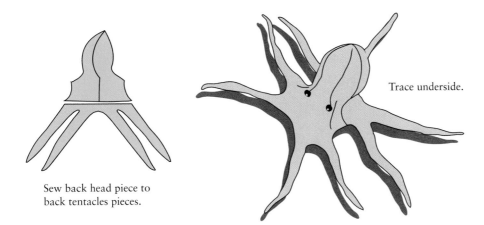

Sew back head piece to
back tentacles pieces.

Trace underside.

MAKING IT

1. Enlarge and photocopy the shapes on the opposite page to use as a pattern. Cut out.

2. Place the front pattern piece on the fabric so that the dotted edge rests along the fold, and cut. Mark the darts on the fabric before unpinning the pattern piece.

3. Sew darts and seams in head. Sew all seams with 3/8" seam allowance.

4. Cut two small ovals for the eyelids out of wool fabric and slightly pull edges to fray a bit. Sew the eyelids in place just below each dart.

5. Sew buttons on top of the ovals for eyes.

6. Cut out two back head pieces and sew center back seam.

7. Place back tentacle pattern piece on fabric so that the dotted edge rests along the fold, and cut.

8. Sew the back head section to the back tentacles.

9. Sew front and back together along side seams.

10. Spread the completed form out on your contrasting fabric and trace so that the underside fits perfectly. Sew the two pieces right sides together, leaving a small opening for stuffing.

11. Turn the octopus right side out and divide beans evenly into each tentacle. This gives the ends some weight and makes the octopus a little floppy.

12. Finish stuffing with polyester and hand sew the opening shut.

Suitcase Coffee Table

BY CAROLINE HUTH

I go to estate sales every weekend and often find old suitcases for under $5 that I can't resist. Usually they are beautiful and solid as a rock, but are just too heavy to be functional for travel these days. Stacking them up as end tables is fine, but I like to make them even more practical by affixing casters to the bottom. They become small rolling tables, perfect for your next soiree.

For a shoebox apartment, one large suitcase can be both your main coffee table and some much-needed storage. For a larger place, several mismatched tables (or, heck, matched and monogrammed) can be grouped together, or even stored under a larger table. The best news is that most of the storage capacity is still intact, so while on top they hold your martinis and caviar, inside you can stash anything you don't want your guests to see.

You'll Need:

I old suitcase (the larger and sturdier the better)

4 pieces of 2" x 4" wood (see instructions below for lengths)

8 wood screws

4 casters, 2-3" long

20 machine screws at least I" long to fit into casters

Saw (or have wood cut at hardware store)

Drill

Screwdriver (or driver bit for drill)

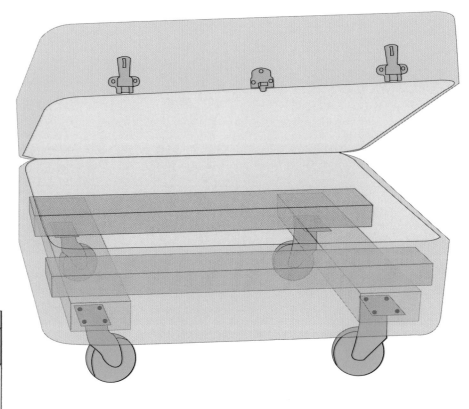

Bottom view   Frame inside suitcase

MAKING IT

1. Open suitcase and lay it flat on a table. If it is a nice, solid hard-sided case then you just need two pieces of 2" x 4" to screw the casters into. If your suitcase is kind of wobbly, you'll want to build a frame inside to screw the casters to, and to stabilize the whole thing a bit. (The suitcases shown needed some stabilization.)

2. Measure the inside dimensions of the suitcase and cut your wood to fit two pieces horizontally and two vertically. Lay two of the pieces of wood down along the edge of the suitcase (see diagram). These will be the ones the casters screw into. Lay the other two pieces perpendicularly across the top and screw them together with two wood screws at each intersection. This is your frame. Do not screw the frame to the suitcase.

3. Turn the suitcase over with the frame in it. If your suitcase is tall, you'll probably notice that the frame isn't as tall as the suitcase sides and wants to fall down to the table below. Since you need to screw into it, put a couple of 2" x 4" scraps underneath it to raise it up nice and tight against the inside of the suitcase. Position your first caster in place and drill holes for the machine screws through the suitcase and into the 2" x 4" below. Then, screw in the machine screws.

4. Repeat for the next three casters.

5. Turn your suitcase over and close the latches. Your coffee table is ready to roll!

More Thrift Store Finds

DOUBLE BOILERS

Back in the day when your mom or your mom's mom used to make dinner every night, a double boiler must have came in handy, as evidenced by the plethora of them residing on the pots-n-pans shelf waiting for a new home. This is great for a crafter because if you're going to screw up a pot trying to pour your own candles (or soap), make your own chocolate or melt plastic for a variety of fun reasons, it's best to do it in a pot that you only paid a buck for.

JEANS

Two words: Rag rugs. They're easy, they're fun (they're also terribly time-consuming, but who's counting hours?) and they're affordable, thanks to the once-fashionable, now-affordable Tapered Jean. Tear up those Gloria Vanderbilts and start braiding, my friends!

DRAPES

Not for hanging, usually, (though consider yourself lucky if you find a set that actually fits your windows AND your decor) but interesting old drapery fabric makes great new pillow fabric. Or table runners. Little cloth bags. You get the idea.

BOARD GAMES

What can't you do with an old board game? Missing pieces are no problem if you plan to cut up the boards anyway. In case you never noticed, game boards are about as thick as a book cover. Also good for portfolios, sturdy little boxes, room dividers (hey you can't divide enough rooms in my book), etc.

WOOL SWEATERS

You can use scraps of old ugly sweaters to make scarves, mittens, slippers, anything warm. It's wool after all. (See Spinning and Recycling Craftshop page 19.) Also, they're perfect for felting projects (see page 82). Look for sweaters with stains you can work around and then bargain with the salespeople.

Wall Murals

BY KIM KRANS

I began to collaborate with friends on walls of our house, tossing around ideas like "maybe the cover of Leonard Cohen 'Songs From A Room' on that wall," or "a Matisse painting up there." This way of working also allows one to become involved directly in the making of the image; instead of framing a bad quality print of a Kandinsky painting, try mimicking those brushstrokes, try finding yourself in that frenzy he was in.

You'll Need:

Photocopy of an image

Interior paint (Benjamin Moore makes a great eco-friendly line of paints that are less toxic and quicker drying than other interior paints)

Brushes

Masking tape or blue painter's tape

A level

A ladder

Pencil and eraser

Acrylic matte medium (available at art supply stores)

Ruler

Level

Selecting your image or idea is of course the most important step. I recommend first-time wall-painters keep it simple. Try finding an image or photograph that is easily reduced to a few colors, or better yet black and white. If you are going to use a photograph, I suggest photocopying it in black and white. You don't want to get involved and overwhelmed by color mixing right away, especially not on the walls of your house. Make sure it is an image or text that you can live with for a while. Album covers, movie posters, lyrics, and your favorite paintings or drawings will be the best source of inspiration for your wall painting. Rummage through your favorite catalogues and books. You may want the specific image or text to have some relationship to the space in which it occupies. Or you may want something simple and abstract, such as vertical rainbow pinstripes, in which case your basic idea and masking tape technique is what counts. After you have chosen your source material, select the best format for displaying your idea. I have simplified the options in to two categories: image (gridding technique) and abstraction (taping technique).

IMAGE PAINTING

For this project I chose to reproduce the cover of Leonard Cohen's "Songs From A Room." A simple and haunting black and white portrait, it has been one of my favorites for a long time now.

MAKING IT

1. Make a few photocopies of your chosen image. Try enlarging or reducing the original to find a size that is easy to work with. I enlarged my picture until it took up nearly the whole 8 1/2" x 11" sheet of paper.

2. Using your ruler and pencil, make a grid covering the photocopied image by making a little mark every 1/2" across the bottom of the paper. Do the same along the side. Line up your ruler with the little marks on opposite sides of the paper and draw lines across the image. This grid will serve as your guide, so the more accurate you are at this stage, the better.

3. Once your grid is drawn, label each square running horizontally with a number and each square running vertically with a letter. This will make your drawing much easier, as you can match up the coordinates and find the tip of the ear at C7 without making any silly mistakes.

4. Next, make a grid on the wall by enlarging your small paper version. You can make your wall painting any size because the grid allows you to replicate the image with accuracy, even if you can't draw well. Once you decide on the approximate size you would like the wall painting to be, calculate how many inches should be represented by the squares of the grid. For instance, I wanted my painting to be about 3' across (36"), so each of the 12 squares on my photocopy represented 3" on the wall. Therefore, I made little marks every 3" on the wall across and then down. Using a long ruler and level, I drew the larger grid on the wall.

5. Label your grid again by lightly penciling in your numerical and alphabetical coordinates just as you did on the photocopy. When drawing on the wall, draw lightly and try to erase with care. A good eraser will also help to avoid smudges.

6. You now have a perfect drawing guide to make your wall painting. You can avoid all of those times in high school art class when you knew there was something "not right about the eyes" in your self-portrait, but you couldn't put your finger on it. Maybe the eyes were too close together, but you had no point of reference allowing you to see this. Now it should be easy to work on areas even as difficult as the eyes, because you no longer have to think about them as eyes, but as shapes within a square. You'll find yourself saying things like, "the left eyebrow ends right before the third square from the right..." or "the top lip runs across four and one-third squares." The success of your replication will depend on your patience and your willingness to try to "see" each individual square for what it's worth and what pictorial information it holds within. Remember to work slowly with good lighting.

(Top to Bottom)
The image with grid.
Grid transferred onto wall.
Drawing image in grid on wall.
Painting the image.
More painting.
You can see the grid in this detail.

7. Now that you have finished the toughest part, pull out your selected paints. Since you have decided to keep it simple and reduce the image to a photocopy, you can now use any two colors (or more if you're adventurous) to represent the black and white areas. I chose white and a pale grey, in order to soften the look of the image. Pour your paints into manageable small containers, and save one container for water. Using larger brushes first, block in the larger areas, leaving the detailed areas for later when you have a better knack for using the paint and brush. Once you have filled in most of the areas, use your small brushes to work on the detailed areas of the picture, painting right up to meet your drawn lines.

8. After your paint is dry, you can go back in and try to deal with the gridded pencil marks that may be still visible. Try to do most of this with an eraser, but you can also touch up with white paint over the pencil, although it may take a few layers. Once you get rid of any signs of the grid, you may not be bothered by a little graphite showing up here or there. After all, there is something nice about seeing a little of the process in the product.

ABSTRACT PAINTING

For this project I chose to make a rainbow-like sunburst on my bedroom wall. The design is inspired by one-point perspective, eclipses, crystals, and time-space travel. I chose a pastel and gray palette.

MAKING IT

1. Once you have an idea for your design (this taping technique lends itself to projects involving stripes and edges), make a few sketches of it on paper, varying the color or scale each time. At first you may think five wide vertical stripes will look best, but after drawing it out you may realize you want fifteen.

2. Clean and lightly dust your wall. Since the success of this project depends so much on the adhesion between the tape and wall, it needs to be as clean as possible.

3. Measure out and mark your design. I wanted the center point of the sunburst to be quite high on the wall in order to emphasize the high ceilings in my bedroom, and I also wanted it to be centered between two walls. Using the pencil, I made a small "x" at this exact point, and used it for reference. Depending on your design, you will have to lightly mark the edges or points in order to match up the tape.

4. Begin taping your design on the wall. Using the center "x" as a guide, I taped and extended one edge of the ray out to the corner of the wall. Then, estimating how thick I wanted the ray, I placed the second length of tape down. You must adhere the tape firmly to the wall, especially on the edges, so as not to allow paint to seep underneath the tape creating a sloppy edge.

5. Paint between the tape. For my design, the most important element was patience. Since the rays of color converge at the center point, each ray had to be painted and then be fairly dry before I could do another.

You'll Need:

Blank paper or sketchbook

Pens or markers

Interior paint

1/2" masking tape (The width of tape you need is determined by the design. The usual blue painter's tape is quite expensive and is not any more useful for this project than regular masking tape.)

Pencil

Eraser

Ruler

Level

A few brushes, both big and small

6. Gently pull off the tape. Have a bag or trash can ready to put the painted tape into, as it can become a messy sticky pile before you know it.

7. Repeat steps 4-6 until your design is finished. You may choose to do all yellow rays first, than all green rays, etc. but you can also mix and match until you have a shape and color scheme you like.

8. Erase any pencil marks or small drips that accumulated along the way.

NOTE: If the edges of your lines are too sloppy for your taste (this will depend on the roughness of your wall as well as the adhesion of the tape), then try this technique:

After you adhere the tape to your wall, paint a thin layer of matte medium (available at art stores) over the seam between the tape and the wall with a brush. This will seal the seam, not allowing paint to seep under the tape. Let it dry and paint as usual. Before removing the tape, run an Exacto blade along the tape's edge. Remove the tape and revel in your perfect edges.

Craftivity Contributors

These are the folks who have contributed not only to the Supernaturale website, but now to *Craftivity*. Meet them. Love them.

JESSE ALEXANDER lives in New York. On Tuesday December 27, 2005 at 11:01 pm he was engaged. Now he's trying to figure out how to make a ton of money so he can send his future kids to a good school. Before he had been idling his time away on projects such as a silk scarf company named www. JeromeJerome.com, a creative agency called www. CrumleyAlexander.com, and a personal site, www. OvertimeAndUnderstand.com, that is never updated.

SUSAN BARBER spent her earliest years in the wilderness of British Columbia. She later graduated from The Cooper Union and continues to work in New York City as a designer of print, packaging, and motion graphics. She lives among plants and cats and dreams of a backyard woodshop shed. She loves dancing in living rooms, sleeping in barns, and sending valentines. Look her up at www.susanbarber.com.

LOGAN BILLINGHAM lives in New York City. Among the heaps of items on her desk you will find: a computer, a sewing machine, a camera, very sharp scissors, super glue, and a stack of unread books.

SCOTT BODENNER is a textile designer in Brooklyn. His fabrics are available in worldwide fabric collections including Maharam, Knoll, Brunschwig and Fils and Grey Watkins. His work is also in the Art Institute of Chicago and the Rhode Island School of Design museum. He is a graduate of Rhode Island School of Design.

DIANE BROMBERG is an artist and a mom with a history of starting and managing innovative businesses. She works with two creative firms, Flat and mgmt. to keep them sailing smoothly. Someday she will get back to Futuregift. Its products are innovative, one-of-a-kind objects, some of which are edible! She is a graduate of Rhode Island School of Design.

JOHANNA BURKE is an artist and craft expert who currently works at Bergdorf Goodman creating celebrated window displays. Her collaborative artworks include the interactive performance/public sculpture piece Sincerely Yours Escorts. The piece consists of 10 uniformed compassionates whose mission statement reads "...to ensure sincerity in the contemporary arts through the professional practice of pleasant conversation and ready availability of free sympathy for all clientele." She has exhibited in New York City with White Columns Gallery, P.S.1 Contemporary Art Center, Creative Time, and The Or Gallery in Vancouver, B.C.

ANNIKA GINSBERG started crafting at the age of six. She learned her love of knitting from a magical woman named Ursula, and she's been crafting ever since. She has a passionate love for fiber of all kinds and has worked as a papermaker as well as teaching knitting for the Church of Craft. And llamas make her laugh.

DESIREE HAIGH currently lives in Seattle with a male companion who always begs her to sleep in just a little bit longer. She is also the craftsonista of *creme*, www.cremery.com, an online shop of all her handmade and vintage wares.

JENNY HART is an artist, author, and founder of Sublime Stitching. She has been an innovator of embroidery since 2000 when she first experimented with stitching. Her works in embroidery have been published and exhibited internationally and are included in the collections of Elizabeth Taylor, Carrie Fisher, and The Roger Miller Museum. Her kits, patterns, and books are sold worldwide. You can find them at www.sublimestitching.com.

KIRSTEN HUDSON is a clutter clearer, feng shui consultant, and all around entrepreneurial explorer. She is currently living in America, but believes the future is Canadian. She can be tapped for work at decluttery.com and many of her personal projects are on display at www.pinkospy.com.

CAROLINE HUTH is a graphic designer and closet crafter in St. Louis, Missouri who lives for estate sales, buys anything old and beat up (and anything in robin's egg blue), and pays way too much attention to her cats.

CALLIE JANOFF is a founding Minister of the Church of Craft (www.churchofcraft.org) and runs the New York City chapter. She makes everything she can get her mitts on. She has an MFA from the School of the Art Institute in Chicago.

GARTH JOHNSON is a ceramic artist who hails from Nebraska, but lives and works in Atlanta, Georgia. He holds a MFA degree from Alfred University, and maintains a ceramics studio in his kitchen. His work can be found online at wondabread.com and www.potteryliberationfront.com. In his spare time, Garth also maintains beloved weblog www.extremecraft.com.

JENNIFER KABAT lives, works, and writes in London and Margaretville, New York. She scribes about architecture and design (among other things) and occasionally advises and writes for big companies. She's decided that writing is a bit like making lace out of very plain old string and in that way is like crafting. Only her craft mistakes often look better and more three-dimensional than her writing errors, which all remain flat on paper.

ANNETTE KESTERSON is a librarian by day, porn-by-numbers maven by night and crazy cat lady through and through. She loves books, buttons and booze and spends more time making things than the average person spends watching the television. All this and more at www.scarletlibrarian.com.

KIM KRANS is an artist living and working in New York City. She loves the city in all of its glory, yet most recently fantasizes about the day she will move in to the backwoods with her closest friends and form a small town that mimics the magical formations of Aurora Borealis.

LANA LÊ is an illustrator and graphic designer with a passion for knitting and crochet. She likes to make things for her husband and two children. See more of her work at www.woolypear.com.

LESLIE LINKSMAN is an interior designer living in Beacon, New York.

DOUG LLOYD met Tsia Carson at an ice cream social when they were 16. He's been madly in love with her ever since. Doug is also a partner at Flat (www.flat.com), a multi-disciplinary design firm founded in 1996 and located in New York City. Flat works with a varied clientele to solve identity, interactive, and editorial design challenges. The practice is predicated on the belief that good design facilitates the smooth flow of information and enlivens all forms of social discourse. Doug earned his MFA from Ohio State University and BFA from Nova Scotia College of Art and Design. He has taught at New York University, Parsons School of Design, University of the Arts, Rhode Island School of Design, and Yale University.

MALAINA NEUMANN headed to a yoga ashram in rural Virginia and ended up with two kids, a husband and a log cabin. She sells a small selection of vintage clothing, which is very reasonably priced, and her own screenprinted/hand appliqued tees from her site www.karmaboutique.com.

HELEN NODDING trained in Fine Art at England's Central Saint Martins College of Art & Design, graduating in 2001. Since then she has lived and worked in London and is currently a Museum Technician at the Victoria and Albert Museum. Whilst at college Helen met and has worked closely ever since with a London-based group called the Spacehijackers, www.spacehijackers.org, who question and critique the use of public space. In 2004 she set up www.storiesfromspace.co.uk as a showcase for her site specific projects and drawings. Helen co-created and now co-edits *Interlude Magazine* (www.interludemagazine.co.uk), a quarterly arts and literary publication.

JESSICA POUNDSTONE creates artistic little color explosions with her Jewelry By Jessica (www.jewelrybyjessica.com) line of necklaces, earrings, and pins. In her spare time, between writing and illustrating assignments, she frequents movie theaters, libraries, concert venues and art galleries, ever on the lookout for new and inspiring ideas.

ANNA RADDATZ grew up in Spokane, Washington, lives in New York City, and works at the Lower East Side Tenement Museum. She dabbles in crochet, sewing, embroidery, sculpture, photography, the Church of Craft, and the study of folk art. She collects rusty metal objects and art made by friends.

DAVID RAINBIRD is cofounder and creative director of Fibre, a British graphic design agency. And while he likes textiles and all kinds of fabric-y, fiberous things, his work is often confined to print and the web. You can see more of it at www.fibre-design.co.uk.

DOUGLAS RICCARDI grew up outside of New York City in a home where there was always some craft project going on: string art, nail art, kachina doll carving, leather crafts, calligraphy, and macramé to name a few. So it's no surprise that his spare time is filled with knitting, furniture making, painting, carving, and general making of stuff. A graduate of Rhode Island School of Design and a professional graphic designer, Douglas created the backgammon board because there were few available that didn't feature brown and tan pleather in horrific proportions. See his firm Memo's work at www.memo-ny.com.

RODGER STEVENS was born in Brooklyn and educated at Parsons School of Design and The School of Visual Arts. His work has been appearing in galleries, museums and publications in the United States and elsewhere since 1993. He has done commissioned work for such clients as The Whitney Museum of Art, The Katonah Museum, The Bristol Museum, Tiffany & Co., Jonathan Adler, Yohji Yamamoto, Stuart Weitzman, The New York Children's Museum of Art, The Federal Reserve Bank of New York, and MTV. Rodger continues to sculpt, draw, take pictures, and live in New York City.

KAREN TANAKA is the Creative Director of Lion Brand Yarn.

NAD THITADILAKA runs a handmade felt accessories company called nFelt (www.nfelt.com). Most nFelt products are created on top of her kitchen counter, to be exact. Nad is originally from Phuket, Thailand, where there is no wool nor snow. She thinks it must be destiny for her to felt.

MEEGHAN TRUELOVE is a writer and adventurer. She lives in the wilds of Brooklyn.

BRETT WEBB has been actively participating in the graffiti scene since 1988. He has painted walls and other objects from the West Coast to Europe and many places in between. While attending the University of Southern California in 1993, Brett became one half of the first website dedicated to graffiti, Art Crimes, at www.graffiti.org, a leading authority of graffiti culture. As well as being featured as a panelist at the Rock and Roll Hall of Fame in Cleveland and part of the selection committee for the Altoids Curiously Strong Graffiti 2002 project committee, he has spoken at conferences and jams in Switzerland, Portugal and throughout the US. Brett currently resides in Brooklyn with his lovely wife Amanda and two huge black cats.

PEARCE WILLIAMS lives in New York and works with a wide variety of media, from painstaking to immediate. While she has a foundation in traditional textiles, she enjoys mingling these practices with contemporary ones, such as stop-motion animation, papier maché, and sculpture/installation to create narrative work that causes us to question our level of comfort with objects that are ordinarily very familiar. She ardently believes that daily life can be made much more sensational through the incorporation of handmade things.

Resources

Websites

SUPERNATURALE
www.Supernaturale.com

SuperNaturale is a site dedicated to the DIY lifestyle in all its wonderful and irreverent handmade formats. Go there to find the patterns from this book, interviews with the contributors, assorted goodies, great how-to articles and a wonderful online community of people on our Glitter boards.

THE CHURCH OF CRAFT
www.Churchofcraft.org

Crafting in groups is a great way to keep on crafting. The Church of Craft is an organization that sees crafting as a spiritual practice. With biweekly craft-ons, the church has chapters across North America and Europe. If there isn't one near you, the church encourages people to start chapters of their own. See the website for more information.

52 PROJECTS
www.52projects.com

This is a great website full of ideas about bringing creativity into your everyday life. Based on the goal of doing a project a week, Jeffrey Yamaguchi provides inspiration for us all.

Showcases

Lexi Boeger's hand spun yarn
Plucky Fluff, www.pluckyfluff.com

Cherokee Hinrich's hand spun yarn
midnightandlulu.etsy.com

Linda Scharf's hand spun yarn
Stone Leaf Moon, www.stoneleafmoon.com

Abigail Doan's crochet snow
AbigailDoan.NeoImages.net

Leslie Baum's paintings
www.bodybuilderandsportsman.com

Deborah Thomas' work
email brokenglass@btinternet.com

Madelon Galland's upholstered tree stumps
www.madelongalland.com

Obadiah Eelcut's Noney
www.noney.net

Other *Showcases* were created by project contributors. See their bios for their websites.

Supplies

Check this list, organized by project, for hard-to-find materials.

KOOL AID DYEING
Crystal Palace
www.straw.com/cpy

POM POM RUG
Brown Sheep
www.brownsheep.com

Lion Brand
www.lionbrand.com

Knit Picks
www.knitpicks.com

METHOD SCARF
Crystal Palace
www.straw.com/cpy

Rowan
www.knitrowan.com

KNIT LAMPSHADE
Lion Brand
www.lionbrand.com

FLOWER BROOCH
See Bedazzled Table Linens

KNIT HAMMOCK
American Hemp
americanhemptwine.com

BEDAZZLED TABLE LINENS
Generic rhinestone setters
www.artcove.com/
Rhinestones/
rhinestones.shtml
www.rhinestones.com/
setter.htm

Crystals
M and J Trim
www.mjtrim.com

JS Beads
www.jsbeads.com/
Swarovski-Crystal/
Swarovski-Flatbacks.asp

Toho Shoji
www.tohoshojiny.com

FELT NECKLACE
Merino wool roving
Mielkes Farm
www.mielkesfarm.com

Necklace Yarn
Habu
www.habutextiles.com

POETIC SILK SCARF
Silk screen kits and supplies
Pearl Paint
www.pearlpaint.com

MOSAIC TRIVETS
For stained glass, eBay is the best.

BLING BLING TEAPOT
Decal paper
Lazertran
www.lazertran.com

Custom ceramic decals
Easy Ceramic Decals
www.easyceramicdecals.com

LIGHTED DISPLAY SHELF
Kirei board
Bettencourt Wood
www.bettencourtwood.com

WALL MURALS
Benjamin Moore Eco Spec® Interior Latex
www.benjaminmoore.com

Craftshop Resources
SPINNING
Handspun Revolution
(self-published)
Lexi Boeger at
www.pluckyfluff.com

KNITTING
The smartest knitting book ever: *Knitting for Anarchists* by Anna Zilboorg (Unicorn Books for Craftsmen Inc., September 2002).

FELTING
For unusual felted pieces (boots, bags, bedspreads, lamps) excellent for inspiration, *Feel* at www.feeldesigned.com.

SILK SCREENING
Although a bit dry, *Printers' National Environmental Assistance Center* (www.pneac.org) is a good resource for silk screening materials and techniques.

WOODWORKING
Find out more about sustainable lumber at www.woodguildsocal.com, www.woodfinder.com and www.certifiedwood.org.

Credits

Craftivity by Tsia Carson

CONTRIBUTING EDITORS
Scott Bodenner
Kirsten Hudson
Karen Tanaka

CONTRIBUTORS
Jesse Alexander
Susan Barber
Logan Billingham
Diane Bromberg
Johanna Burke
Annika Ginsberg
Desiree Haigh
Jenny Hart
Caroline Huth
Callie Janoff
Garth Johnson
Jennifer Kabat
Annette Kesterson
Kim Krans

Lana Lê
Leslie Linksman
Doug Lloyd
Malaina Neumann
Helen Nodding
Jessica Poundstone
Anna Raddatz
David Rainbird
Douglas Riccardi
Rodger Stevens
Nad Thitadilaka
Meeghan Truelove
Brett Webb
Pearce Williams

SHOWCASES
Leslie Baum
Lexi Boeger
Abigail Doan
Obadiah Eelcut

Madelon Galland
Cherokee Hinrichs
Linda Scharf
Deborah Thomas

MAKERS
Amanda Cooper
Tatiana Ginsberg
Holly Gressley
Mary Izetelny
Beverly Joel
Justin Laman
Kathryn McGowan
Kate Meacham
Mitsue Tanaka
Allyson Vermeulen
Dave Williams
Jeffrey Yamaguchi

DONORS
American Hemp
Benjamin Moore
Bettencourt Green
  Lumberyard
Brown Sheep Yarns
Crystal Palace Yarns
Knit Picks Yarns
Lion Brand Yarns
Rowan Yarns

Art Direction & Design Flat
This book is set in Priori and Sabon

Photography Svend Lindbaek
(except where noted)

Photography of projects in process, in enviroments, on models, and monkeys Flat
Additional photography Jesse Alexander (p. 97, 204), Tim Barber (p. 184-188), Greg Barth (p. 209), Jamie Daughters (p. 167), Brian Crumley (p. 109), Abigail Doan (p. 56), Madelon Galland (p. 179), Garth Johnson (p. 153, 159), Kim Krans (p. 215), Karen Tanaka (p. 17, 19, 26-30, 40-44, 171-172), Nad Thitadilaka (p. 88), and Deborah Thomas (p. 139).
Models Erin Kaleel, Doug Lloyd, Cedar Lloyd
Hand Model Callie Janoff

Special Thanks
Nick Darrell, Anne Cole and Mary Ellen O'Neill at HarperCollins, Robin Dellabough at Lark Productions. This book could not have been created without their incredible help.

A huge thanks to all the contributors for sharing their work, spending their time, and being very patient with me. The Church of Craft, Phil Conway, Cooper Union wood shop staff (Dave Karlin, Frank Kurtzke, and John Roche), Jamie Daughters, Patrick Daughters, Annette Ferrara, G & G Woodworks, Sister Diane Gilleland, Holly Gressley, John and Susan Hogshead, Helena Keeffe, Aviva Michaelov, Zoë Sheehan Saldaña, Ana Voog, Inga Weiss, and William Stranger Furniture. Of course the Glitterati, especially the beloved mods. And my loving husband Doug.